Strategic Moves

Unlocking Success Through the Science of Game Theory

by
Dylan Kordis

Dylan Kordis

Copyright 2024 Dylan Kordis. All Rights reserved. No part of this publication may be reproduced without consent of the author.

"Game theory is a set of tools used to help analyze situations where an individual's best course of action depends on what others do or are expected to do. Game theory allows us to understand how people act in situations where they are interconnected."

— Ivan Pastine

Dylan Kordis

Table of Contents

Chapter 1: The Games We Play—An Introduction to Game Theory

Chapter 2: The Prisoner's Dilemma—Trust and Betrayal

Chapter 3: Zero-Sum and Non-Zero-Sum Games—Winning Together or Alone

Chapter 4: Nash Equilibrium—Finding Balance Among Competing Interests

Chapter 5: Coordination Games—Achieving Harmony

Chapter 6: The Ultimatum Game—Fairness and Negotiation

Chapter 7: Sequential Games and Backward Induction—Thinking Ahead

Chapter 8: Auctions and Bidding Strategies—Playing for Keeps

Chapter 9: Evolutionary Game Theory—Survival of the Fittest Strategies

Chapter 10: Applying Game Theory in Everyday Life—Becoming a Strategic Thinker

Introduction

In a world where choices shape our destinies, understanding the art of strategic thinking can be the difference between success and missed opportunities. Every day, we face decisions that ripple through our lives, affecting our relationships, careers, and personal growth. But what if you could approach these decisions with the precision of a master chess player, anticipating moves and crafting optimal outcomes?

"Strategic Moves" invites you to step into a realm where everyday choices become powerful tools for shaping your future. Imagine negotiating a salary increase with the confidence of knowing exactly how your boss will respond. Picture navigating complex family dynamics with the finesse of a skilled diplomat. These aren't far-fetched scenarios—they're the real-world applications of game theory, a field that's often misunderstood as purely academic but is, in fact, deeply relevant to our daily lives.

Through relatable stories and practical examples, we'll explore how strategic thinking can transform the way you interact with the world. You'll discover that you're already engaged in strategic decision-making, often without realizing it. Whether you're planning a surprise party or closing a business deal, the principles of game theory are at play.

As we journey through this book, you'll gain insights that will reshape your approach to problem-solving and decision-making. You'll learn to recognize patterns in behavior, anticipate others' actions, and make choices that lead to mutually beneficial outcomes. This isn't about manipulation or outsmarting others—it's about understanding the structures that underpin our interactions and using that knowledge to foster cooperation and success.

Get ready to unlock the power of strategic thought. By the time you finish "Strategic Moves," you'll view your world through a new lens, equipped with tools to navigate life's complexities with confidence and skill. Let's begin this transformative journey together.

Dylan Kordis

Chapter 1: The Games We Play—An Introduction to Game Theory

The Origins of Strategy in Human History

The idea of strategy has been around for as long as humans have existed. It's not just limited to battles and games of chess; it's part of every interaction we have. To understand where strategic thinking comes from, we need to take a trip back in time, exploring different eras and cultures. This journey shows us how the need to plan and predict the actions of others arose as a way to survive.

Let's think about early hunter-gatherer societies. In these small groups, each person had to make decisions that could mean life or death. Every hunt came with a lot of choices: Should someone chase after a herd of deer heading to the river, or should they stay behind to protect the spot where berries might soon be ready to pick? Each decision meant weighing risks and rewards, not just for themselves but for the entire group. Those early humans were unknowingly playing the first versions of game theory, where the stakes were high and the outcomes could mean the difference between survival and disaster.

Now, let's fast forward to ancient civilizations, where the idea of strategy became even more refined. The ancient Greeks were not only great thinkers but also skilled tacticians. They looked deeply into how people make decisions and how those choices impact the group. Sun Tzu's "The Art of War," written in the 5th century BC, goes beyond just military strategy. It teaches us the importance of knowing our opponents, predicting their actions, and using our strengths to counter their weaknesses. This work still resonates today, showing us that strategic thinking has always been relevant.

As societies grew, so did the complexity of their strategic games. The rise of empires brought new layers, where diplomacy and negotiation became just as important as fighting on the battlefield. The Romans knew that sometimes the best approach was to avoid direct conflict. Instead, they focused on forming alliances that could help them deal with threats. The ability to build coalitions and nurture relationships is a key part of strategic thinking, still seen in modern business and politics.

The Renaissance was another turning point. During this time, strategic thinking began to mesh with new scientific ideas. Thinkers like Niccolò Machiavelli, in his book "The Prince," talked about political strategy, focusing on manipulation and foresight. Machiavelli's ideas about power and human behavior still shape how we understand leadership and governance today, highlighting his lasting influence on strategy.

In the 20th century, game theory formally emerged as a mathematical field, gathering ideas that strategists had been using intuitively for ages. John von Neumann and Oskar Morgenstern's book, "Theory of Games and Economic Behavior," laid the groundwork for understanding strategic interactions in a structured way. Their work connected abstract math concepts to real-life applications, impacting fields like economics, evolutionary biology, and psychology.

The development of strategy over the years shows how it threads through cultures and contexts. Strategy is, in many ways, a reflection of human nature—a mix of anticipation and response, cooperation and competition. Whether in the boardroom, on the battlefield, or even at home, strategic thinking helps us navigate the complexities of our relationships.

In our everyday lives, we engage in strategic thinking without even being aware of it. Every choice we make—like negotiating a salary, picking a restaurant with friends, or planning a family getaway—is influenced by our understanding of what others want and how they might react. Recognizing these strategic elements in our daily decisions can not only improve our choices but also enhance our interactions with others.

Understanding the history of strategy gives us valuable insights into the principles of game theory. It reminds us that while our circumstances may change, the basic dynamics of human interaction stay the same. As we explore the finer points of strategic decision-making, we draw on a rich history of thought and practice that stretches back thousands of years.

As we go through various situations in life, it becomes clear that strategic thinking isn't just for economics or politics; it's part of our everyday lives. The ability to predict how others might act, frame our choices around possible outcomes, and create strategies that benefit everyone is a skill we can develop. By embracing the basics of game theory, we can approach daily challenges in a new way, seeing interactions as chances for cooperation and win-win solutions.

The lessons from history also highlight the need to adapt. Just as ancient empires changed their strategies in response to new challenges, we also need to be flexible, allowing us to respond effectively to the ever-changing environments we face. Each interaction is like a mini-game, where our decisions and those of others create a continuous loop of strategy, response, and adjustment.

In today's world, the stakes may look different from the ancient battles or political strategies of the past, but the core of strategy remains unchanged. The negotiations in modern corporate boardrooms echo the alliances and rivalries of past empires. The games of chance and skill we play, from poker nights to business deals, use the same strategic principles that have guided humanity for centuries. By recognizing this connection, we can intentionally weave strategic thinking into our lives, improving our ability to make choices that not only benefit us but also promote cooperation and understanding with those around us.

In the end, the journey from our ancestors' basic instincts to the complex strategies of today highlights the importance of game theory in our lives. It's more than just an academic subject; it's a practical toolkit for navigating the ups and downs of human relationships. By grasping the art of strategy, we unlock the door to better awareness, improved decision-making, and the chance to build connections that go beyond simple transactions. As we step into the world of game theory, we embrace a legacy of ideas that encourages us to engage thoughtfully and strategically with the world around us, creating a more connected and harmonious existence.

Anatomy of a Game

When we think about games, we might imagine sports, board games, or even video games. But the true essence of a game goes much deeper than these familiar activities. At its heart, game theory looks at strategic interactions—those moments when our choices are influenced not just by what we want, but also by what we think others will do. Understanding the anatomy of a game is key to unpacking the details of game theory. It helps us pinpoint the essential parts that shape how decisions are made in a strategic setting.

To really get a feel for how games work, we first need to identify who the players are. In game theory, players aren't just athletes competing in a match. They can be individuals, groups, organizations, or even entire countries. Each player comes to the game with their own preferences, resources, and goals. This variety adds layers of complexity to decision-making. For example, two companies competing for market share might take very different approaches based on their unique strengths, financial situations, and future ambitions.

Next, let's think about the strategies players use. A strategy is essentially a game plan that a player follows in response to what they anticipate others will do. In a competitive environment, players carefully consider the possible choices of their rivals, aiming to pick a strategy that will give them the best results. Here, we find an important distinction in game theory: cooperative versus non-cooperative games.

In cooperative games, players can make binding agreements and work together to improve their outcomes. Imagine a group of friends deciding where to eat; they talk about their preferences and come to a decision that makes everyone happy. On the flip side, non-cooperative games operate under different rules. In these situations, players act on their own, making decisions based purely on their self-interest, even if working together would lead to better results. Think of an auction where each bidder tries to outsmart the others without discussing their strategies.

As we dig a bit deeper into the anatomy of a game, we come across the concept of payoffs. Payoffs are the results players get from their chosen strategies. These outcomes can take many forms—money, points in a game, or even personal satisfaction. The way payoffs are structured is crucial in shaping how players decide what to do. For example, in a simple game of rock-paper-scissors, the payoffs are clear-cut: a win, loss, or draw. But in more complicated scenarios, like a corporate merger, payoffs can be tied to many factors, such as market share, employee retention, and brand reputation.

Timing also plays a big role in decision-making within games. Players can make their moves at the same time or take turns, leading to different strategic dynamics. In simultaneous games, players choose their strategies without knowing what others have picked—just like in rock-paper-scissors. Here, players must weigh their options carefully, thinking about what their opponents might do before they make their move.

In sequential games, on the other hand, players take turns making decisions, which allows each person to see the previous moves before deciding on their own. This setup adds a layer of anticipation and lets players adjust their strategies based on what others have done. A great example of this is chess, where each player must consider not just their opponent's immediate moves but also their long-term strategies.

As we break down the anatomy of a game, we also need to look at dominant strategies. A dominant strategy is one that ensures a player gets a better outcome no matter what the others choose. Imagine a job seeker whose qualifications are a perfect match for a position. This candidate might stick to the same application strategy—tailoring their resume and preparing thoroughly for interviews—regardless of what other candidates are doing. Often, spotting a dominant strategy can simplify decisions, allowing players to focus on one best approach that maximizes their payoff.

Yet, the world of game theory isn't always so straightforward. This is where the

Nash equilibrium comes in, adding a more intricate layer to strategic interactions. Named after mathematician John Nash, the Nash equilibrium occurs when players reach a point where no one can gain by changing their strategy on their own, given what everyone else is doing. In other words, each player has found their best strategy based on the choices of others. This balance shows how interconnected player strategies are and highlights the need to predict what others will do.

To illustrate this concept, let's take a look at a classic example: the Prisoner's Dilemma. In this situation, two criminals are caught and placed in separate rooms. They face the choice of either staying silent or betraying each other by confessing. If both stay silent, they receive a light sentence. If one betrays while the other stays silent, the betrayer goes free while the silent one gets a heavy sentence. If both betray each other, they both get moderate sentences. The Nash equilibrium comes into play when both players decide to betray each other, as neither can improve their outcome by changing their strategy on their own. Even though they could achieve a better result through cooperation, the fear of betrayal leads them to make the less desirable choice.

This example highlights the complexities and contradictions that can come with strategic decision-making. Game theory gives us a way to analyze these situations and gain a better understanding of the principles that drive human interactions. By breaking down the anatomy of a game—players, strategies, payoffs, and timing—we can see how these elements come together to create complex webs of decision-making.

As we explore the different uses of game theory in the following sections, this foundational knowledge will be really helpful. Whether we're looking at economic behavior, political negotiations, or personal relationships, the ideas we gather from the anatomy of a game will shine a light on the strategies in play and help us make better decisions.

What's fascinating about game theory is how it applies to so many different areas. From the boardroom to a poker game, the same strategic principles shape our interactions. By understanding the components of a game, we give ourselves the power to engage more thoughtfully with the world around us. As we continue to explore the intricacies of strategic thinking, let's welcome the challenge of anticipating the moves of others while crafting our own strategies to achieve the best outcomes. Whether we're cooperating, competing, or trying to balance the two, the skills we develop through studying game theory will enhance our ability to navigate the complexities of life and relationships.

Everyday Games

Life can often feel like we're constantly playing different games—some are fun, while others are a bit more serious. Each day, we find ourselves negotiating, planning, and sometimes competing in ways that reflect the ideas behind game theory. Think about the last time you tried to negotiate at a car dealership. The playful back-and-forth with the salesperson, the knowing looks exchanged, and the mental math you do to figure out your budget—all these moments are part of a larger game of strategic decision-making. When we start to notice these patterns, we can appreciate just how universal game theory really is.

Picture this: you're shopping for a new family car. You've done your homework, created a list of what you need, and even worked out your budget to the last penny. But the moment you step onto the dealership lot, it feels like you've entered a whole new world. The salesperson approaches with a friendly smile, ready to engage in a strategic dance. You know what you want, but so do they. The game is on, with both of you aiming for different goals.

In this game, you have opposing strategies. The salesperson wants to maximize their commission, nudging you toward pricier options, while trying to offer you the smallest discount possible. Meanwhile, you just want a dependable car that fits your budget without feeling cheated. The stakes are high as both of you strive for the best possible outcome. Each move you make is based not only on your wants but also on what you think the other person will do. For instance, when you offer a lower price, the salesperson might respond with an even higher price, hoping to throw you off balance.

This back-and-forth creates an interesting dynamic, almost like a dance: you step forward, they pull back, and sometimes both of you pause to reassess. Negotiation is a daily game where understanding the strategies at play can lead to better outcomes for both sides. Once you recognize these tactics, you can adjust your approach, boosting your chances of getting what you want while keeping the conversation friendly—a true win-win.

These everyday encounters aren't just about big purchases; they pop up in our daily lives, from planning family vacations to navigating social events and workplace interactions. Think about organizing a family trip. You gather everyone around the dinner table with a list of vacation spots. Each family member has their own preferences—some want to soak up the sun on a beach, while others dream of mountain adventures. In this case, the game shifts again, as you have to balance everyone's interests and desires.

To reach a happy outcome, you might suggest a compromise. Perhaps you propose a destination that offers both a beach and hiking trails, or you could split the trip into two parts so everyone gets a taste of what they want. This teamwork doesn't just reflect good game theory principles; it also strengthens family bonds. Everyone feels valued, and by recognizing the strategies at play, you create a sense of partnership instead of competition.

However, not every game is about competition. A common misunderstanding is that game theory only applies when people are at odds. This misconception can result in missed chances for collaboration, especially in situations where teamwork is crucial. Take a workplace environment, for example. Employees need to work together to reach shared goals, but individual ambitions can sometimes create tension.

Let's say a team has a project due soon. Each member brings unique skills and viewpoints, creating an exciting but challenging mix. The trick is aligning these different interests toward a common goal. Here, the game is more about cooperation, where finding a win-win scenario is not just better but necessary for success. When team members openly share their strengths and weaknesses, they can craft strategies that make the most of everyone's abilities, leading to a much better outcome than if they all acted alone.

As you process these scenarios, it becomes clear that understanding the strategic elements in our daily lives helps us make smarter choices. Game theory provides a way to see these dynamics, letting us anticipate how others might act and respond in kind. The next time you find yourself negotiating or working together with others, think about the principles of game theory. Ask yourself: What do I want? What do they want? How can we both get what we need?

Let's also touch on another key aspect of game theory: trust. Trust is crucial in cooperative games. If trust is lacking, you might find yourself in situations like the Prisoner's Dilemma, where people act purely out of self-interest instead of working together for mutual gain. In a family, if kids don't believe their parents will consider their preferences, they may feel forced to negotiate harder or keep their thoughts to themselves. This reluctance can undermine the essence of cooperation, leading to outcomes that don't benefit anyone.

In a workplace, trust can greatly influence team dynamics. When team members trust each other, they're more likely to share information openly, collaborate, and engage in productive discussions that spark creativity. On the flip side, a lack of trust can shut down communication and create a toxic atmosphere where individuals prioritize their own interests over the team's goals. By understanding the importance of trust as part of the strategic landscape, we can foster healthier relationships both at home and work.

Now, let's explore some practical ways to apply these ideas in our daily lives. First and foremost, being aware is key. Start paying attention to the interactions around you—how decisions are made, how negotiations play out, and how different interests are balanced. This increased awareness will improve your understanding of the strategic elements involved and help you spot opportunities for cooperation instead of competition.

You might also consider keeping a journal to track your thoughts and observations about everyday games. This can help you consolidate what you've learned and sharpen your strategic thinking skills over time. Write about situations where you successfully navigated a negotiation or missed a chance to collaborate. Reflect on what went well, what didn't, and how you might handle similar situations differently in the future.

Another helpful approach is practicing active listening. In any negotiation or collaborative environment, truly hearing what others say can provide valuable insights into their interests and motivations. When you engage in active listening, you build trust and create a space for open communication, which fosters cooperation. This not only helps you work well with others but also positions you as a strategic thinker who can handle complex interactions smoothly.

Lastly, don't hesitate to seek feedback. Whether you're negotiating a deal or planning a family getaway, inviting feedback from those involved can reveal new paths for collaboration and highlight perspectives you might have overlooked. Embracing feedback can lead to innovative solutions that satisfy everyone and foster a sense of shared ownership over the results.

In the end, recognizing the strategic elements in our daily interactions can change how we make decisions. By applying game theory concepts to the everyday games we play, we become more aware of our choices, the interests of others, and the opportunities for collaboration. The key takeaway is this: life is a series of strategic moves, and by sharpening our understanding of these dynamics, we can navigate the complexities of human interactions with confidence and skill.

As you move forward, challenge yourself to be a more strategic thinker in your personal and professional life. Observe the games around you and draw inspiration from the principles of cooperation, negotiation, and trust. Engage in conversations, explore compromises, and be flexible with your strategies based on the situation. Remember, each interaction is a chance to learn, grow, and create outcomes that benefit everyone involved.

By understanding and applying game theory principles, you're not just playing the game; you're mastering it. So, whether you're trying to negotiate a better price on that dream car, planning the ideal family vacation, or collaborating on a workplace project, keep your strategic mindset sharp. Watch how your choices create positive ripples in your life and the lives of those around you. Ultimately, the beauty of these everyday games lies in the potential for connection, teamwork, and collective success, reminding us that strategic thinking can elevate even the simplest interactions into something truly meaningful.

Dylan Kordis

Chapter 2: The Prisoner's Dilemma—Trust and Betrayal

Classic Conundrum: Understanding the Prisoner's Dilemma

Picture this: you and your partner in crime have been caught and arrested. The police don't have enough proof to pin the main charge on you, but they're giving you a tempting offer. If you decide to turn on your accomplice and testify against them, you can walk free while your partner faces a heavy sentence. On the flip side, if your accomplice betrays you first, they go free while you take the fall. If you both choose to stay quiet, you'll both only get a short sentence for a lesser charge. The situation is intense, and the choice feels like a no-brainer.

This scenario perfectly illustrates something called the Prisoner's Dilemma, a key idea in game theory that shows the clash between acting in your own best interest and the greater good. At the core of this dilemma is an intriguing contradiction: when both players act selfishly, they often wind up worse off than if they had worked together. This paradox highlights a fundamental truth of human behavior—self-preservation can sometimes lead to mutual ruin. It reminds us of the delicate balance between trust and betrayal that we navigate daily, affecting our choices and the bonds we create.

Understanding this tricky situation isn't just an academic exercise; it has real-life implications. The Prisoner's Dilemma shows up in many areas, from how businesses negotiate to international relations, from family decision-making to how we engage with our communities. It urges us to think deeply about our values and the choices we make, pushing us to examine how we pursue our goals while navigating the often cloudy waters of trust and betrayal.

To really appreciate the importance of the Prisoner's Dilemma, we should dive into its story. The classic tale features two suspects, often named Alice and Bob. After being arrested together, they're placed in separate interrogation rooms, unaware of what the other is doing. The police present the same deal to both: betray your partner and walk free, or stay silent and risk a longer sentence. If both keep quiet, they each serve just one year for a minor offense. But if one betrays while the other stays silent, the one who betrays walks free, leaving the silent partner with a harsh ten-year sentence. If both betray each other, they end up with five years in prison.

Now we're faced with a dilemma. Logically, the best choice for each person, considering what the other might do, is to betray. This choice minimizes personal risk, ensuring that they don't end up on the losing side of a bad decision. But if both opt for betrayal, they end up worse off than if they had cooperated. This brings up an important question: why do people often choose betrayal when mutual cooperation would lead to a better outcome?

The answer lies in the uncertainty of the situation. Each person has to weigh their options, thinking about what the other might do while also fighting their instinct for self-preservation. This is similar to many real-life scenarios where trust is fragile. The fear of being taken advantage of often makes people put their interests first, even at the expense of everyone's benefit. At its core, this dilemma highlights a key aspect of human nature: the struggle between cooperation and competition.

Beyond theory, the Prisoner's Dilemma has real-world applications. In business, for instance, companies often find themselves in similar situations. Imagine two competing businesses considering whether to lower their prices. If both lower their prices, they could hurt their profit margins. However, if one lowers its prices while the other holds steady, the one that cut prices could gain a significant market share. The dilemma becomes clear: the decision to cut prices is much like betrayal in the original tale. Trust and cooperation could lead to a healthier market for everyone, yet the fear of being undersold pushes businesses to act in their own interests.

In our personal relationships, trust and betrayal play out in much the same way. Friends often have to decide whether to keep a secret. The anxiety that one might spill the beans for their own benefit can create a divide that pulls them apart. This dilemma shines a light on the struggles of maintaining trust in uncertain times. The possibility of betrayal looms over us, impacting our interactions and decisions in ways we often don't recognize.

As we dig deeper into the Prisoner's Dilemma, it's vital to see that this situation isn't just a theoretical puzzle. It's a recurring issue in human relationships, showcasing the fragile balance between acting in our own interests and considering the greater good. The battle between trust and betrayal influences our decisions and shapes outcomes in ways that often go unnoticed. By exploring the details of this dilemma, we can gain insight into our behavior and the motivations that drive us.

In a world where interactions are unavoidable, the lessons from the Prisoner's Dilemma help us better understand negotiation, cooperation, and competition. Recognizing the factors that shape our choices allows us to approach situations more mindfully, creating an environment where collaboration can flourish. While navigating these complicated scenarios, we must ask ourselves: how can we build trust, reduce betrayal, and ultimately choose paths that benefit not just ourselves but everyone around us?

Looking at how the Prisoner's Dilemma plays out in different situations shows just how relevant it is. Take climate change, for instance. When countries tackle this global issue, they face a version of the dilemma. Each nation has to choose whether to prioritize its own interests by polluting freely or to work together by embracing sustainable practices, even if it costs them economically in the short term. The best outcome comes from collective action, where everyone contributes to solving the problem. However, the worry that others might not hold up their end often leads to a standstill, leaving all nations suffering from environmental harm.

The dilemma also echoes in the world of social media. In a space where information spreads quickly, individuals face choices between sharing genuine content or giving in to the lure of sensationalism. The desire for attention can erode trust within online communities. Each person must choose: do they betray the collective good for individual gain, or do they help foster a culture of authenticity that benefits everyone? The ripple effects of these choices influence not just personal reputations but also the trustworthiness of the platforms themselves.

As we continue to explore the layers of the Prisoner's Dilemma, we must also recognize the vital role of communication in alleviating its challenges. Open and honest conversations can help build trust between individuals, encouraging cooperation even when uncertainty looms. When people feel confident that their interests will be respected, they are more likely to work together, leading to better outcomes for all involved. Essentially, effective communication acts as a bridge over the trust gap the dilemma often creates.

Furthermore, the idea of repeated interactions changes how the dilemma plays out. In one-time scenarios, betrayal might seem like the smart choice, but in ongoing games, people know their actions will have consequences beyond just one encounter. Reputation comes into play, prompting individuals to consider the long-term benefits of working together versus the short-term temptation to betray. In these situations, strategies evolve, and people tend to favor maintaining trust, creating a collaborative environment that ultimately brings greater rewards.

The implications of the Prisoner's Dilemma stretch far beyond individual choices; they weave into the very fabric of society. Understanding these dilemmas helps organizations, communities, and nations establish frameworks that promote cooperation and build trust. By nurturing environments that prioritize collective interests over personal gain, we unlock the potential for collaborative solutions to the challenges we face.

Reflecting on the lessons from the Prisoner's Dilemma, it's clear that navigating the dance of trust and betrayal is something we engage with daily. Whether we're in a boardroom, around the family dinner table, or on the global stage, the choices we make ripple far beyond our immediate situations. The power of working together lies not just in the benefits we gain, but also in the relationships we build along the way.

By embracing the complexity of human interactions, we deepen our understanding of our motivations and the decisions we encounter. The Prisoner's Dilemma offers a mirror to our struggles and victories in the realm of trust. As we take this journey of exploration, we equip ourselves with the tools needed to balance self-interest with the common good, paving the way for a world where cooperation thrives.

Real-World Dilemmas: The Prisoner's Dilemma in Everyday Life

Life is a beautiful mess, constantly presenting us with choices that can either uplift our communities or cater to our own selfish desires. This idea of choice is perfectly illustrated by the Prisoner's Dilemma, a concept that reaches far beyond academic theories and becomes a part of our everyday experiences. From the boardrooms of major companies to the heart of our personal relationships, the lessons from this dilemma play a crucial role in shaping how we interact with one another.

Let's first look at the business world, a vivid place where the Prisoner's Dilemma often plays out. Picture two competing airlines trying to attract the same customers. Each airline faces a tough decision: should they drop their prices to lure in more passengers, or stick to their current rates and risk losing customers to their rival? It seems like a clear choice, but the situation is much more complicated, similar to the tough choice faced by the two prisoners in the classic scenario.

Here's a closer look. If both airlines decide to cut their prices, they enter a dangerous price war that could hurt their profits and leave both worse off. On the flip side, if one airline lowers its prices while the other keeps them steady, the one with the lower prices could grab a bigger slice of the market, boosting their revenue at the expense of their competitor. This situation brings in the tension of betrayal: a seemingly smart choice that could end up being harmful for everyone involved.

Consider what happened in the airline industry after the September 11 attacks in the early 2000s. Airlines faced a crisis like never before. In their rush to reclaim lost customers, many opted for steep discounts. This scenario became a textbook example of the Prisoner's Dilemma. While the lower fares attracted customers temporarily, the long-term effects were dire. Many airlines couldn't keep up with these low prices, leading to financial struggles and even bankruptcies. The initial urge to abandon fair pricing resulted in suffering for many.

Another great example of the Prisoner's Dilemma is seen in the tech world. Companies like Apple and Samsung navigate a tricky landscape where they need to innovate while still making profits. When it comes to launching new products, both companies must choose: should they invest heavily in research to create something groundbreaking or rush to release a mediocre product just to stay ahead? If both companies opt for the latter, they risk drowning in a sea of sameness, missing out on more innovative competitors. However, if one company takes the plunge and invests in innovation, while the other doesn't, the one that takes the risk could win over loyal customers and dominate the market.

Take the rise of touch-screen technology in smartphones. When Apple introduced the iPhone, they set a whole new standard. Initially, Samsung hesitated to invest deeply in touch-screen tech, but soon realized that failing to innovate would cost them market share. This led to a rush of investments in research and development, resulting in the Galaxy series, which not only rivaled but often outperformed Apple's products. Here, the classic dilemma of cooperation versus betrayal unfolds, with high stakes that significantly impact the industry.

Beyond the business realm, the Prisoner's Dilemma is also deeply intertwined with environmental issues. Climate change highlights the struggles of working together as a global community. Countries everywhere grapple with the question: should they cooperate to tackle climate change, even if it means sacrificing short-term economic gains? The consequences of this choice are enormous and will affect generations to come.

Look at the Paris Agreement. It represents a global effort to reduce greenhouse gas emissions, but not all countries are on the same page. Many commit to cutting emissions, yet there's always the fear that some won't do their part. If one country puts its economy first and doesn't cooperate, it could benefit from the efforts of those that do. This creates a real-life version of the Prisoner's Dilemma, where worries about betrayal lead to inaction, making the crisis even worse.

The United States and China often find themselves at odds over these issues. Even though both acknowledge the urgency of addressing climate change, their approaches reveal a struggle between national interests and global responsibility. The saying, "I'll go green if you do," perfectly sums up the dilemma. While working together produces the best results, the fear of taking the initiative alone often hinders progress, leaving the planet and its people vulnerable to the effects of a warming climate.

Interpersonal relationships are another area where trust and betrayal come into play. Our daily interactions often echo the choices faced by those two prisoners. Imagine two close friends who have shared sensitive secrets. One friend has to choose: keep the secret or share it for social gain. If one friend betrays the other's trust while the other stays loyal, the betrayer might gain short-term approval, but they risk losing a valuable friendship. If both decide to hold on to their confidences, they build a stronger bond, reinforcing the idea that trust is vital for meaningful relationships.

Family dynamics show similar patterns. Parents often grapple with whether to confront a child's bad behavior or let it slide for the sake of peace. The fear of pushing the child away can lead to inaction. However, if one parent enforces rules while the other remains lenient, conflict can arise, damaging communication. The Prisoner's Dilemma is evident here, highlighting the importance of cooperation in cultivating strong family ties while also illustrating the risks of betrayal.

Romantic relationships reveal yet another side to the Prisoner's Dilemma. Trust and communication are crucial, but the desire to protect oneself can lead to misunderstandings and resentment. Couples often find themselves in situations where honesty might hurt feelings in the short term, tempting one partner to keep quiet instead of speaking up. If both partners hide their feelings, the relationship can lose its authenticity. However, when they communicate openly, it builds trust, helping them tackle challenges together and strengthening their connection.

At its heart, the Prisoner's Dilemma teaches us that our choices in different areas are interconnected. The fear of betrayal can make us defensive, while the potential for collaboration can enhance our relationships, our environments, and even our economies. The challenge is recognizing these patterns and finding ways to create an atmosphere where trust can thrive.

Encouraging communication can be an effective way to address the dilemmas we face. Honest conversations allow us to explore mutual interests, leading to collaborative solutions. When we engage in open dialogue, we reduce the uncertainty that often leads to betrayal. By fostering a culture of transparency—in business, politics, or personal life—we create an environment that encourages cooperation over selfishness.

We also need to consider the impact of repeated interactions. Unlike one-time encounters, ongoing relationships compel us to think about the long-term effects of our choices. In business, companies that focus on building their reputations are likely to earn trust from consumers and partners. Over time, this trust becomes a valuable asset, contributing to lasting success and a cooperative market.

In personal relationships, the same principle applies. Recognizing that our actions have consequences beyond the immediate moment encourages us to act with integrity. When trust is built, the rewards of cooperation far outweigh the temporary benefits of betrayal. Thus, the dynamics of the Prisoner's Dilemma shift, transforming our interactions into a landscape where collective interests take priority.

In summary, the Prisoner's Dilemma serves as a powerful tool for understanding the many choices we face every day. Whether in business, environmental issues, or personal relationships, the struggle between self-interest and the greater good is always present. By recognizing the delicate balance between trust and betrayal, we can equip ourselves to make better decisions.

Navigating the complexities of human interaction requires us to consciously choose cooperation over competition. By promoting open communication and nurturing a trusting environment, we can create collaborative solutions to the challenges we encounter, both individually and collectively. The lessons from the Prisoner's Dilemma resonate deeply in our everyday lives, guiding us toward more satisfying relationships and a more harmonious world.

Building Cooperation: Strategies to Overcome the Dilemma

In the complex world of social interactions, the rhythm of cooperation often stumbles. We frequently find ourselves torn between the temptation of personal gain and the need for collective benefit. This internal struggle is at the heart of the Prisoner's Dilemma, where cooperation is crucial for mutual success, yet the lure of selfish choices hangs over us like a shadow, promising immediate rewards. To successfully navigate this tricky landscape, we need to adopt strategies that encourage cooperation, helping us break through the barriers set by self-interest.

The first step toward cooperation is building a foundation of trust. Trust may seem elusive, but it's a vital part of our interactions. It acts like armor, shielding us against the risks of betrayal. When people trust one another, they create a welcoming space for collaboration. Consider business partnerships, for example. Companies that take the time to foster trust with their employees, customers, and investors are far more likely to enjoy fruitful collaborations. Trust decreases uncertainty; when you believe your partner will act in good faith, the risk of betrayal fades away, opening the doors to joint ventures and shared successes.

So, how do we nurture this trust? The answer lies in being transparent. Whether in our personal lives or at work, being open about our intentions, goals, and expectations lays the groundwork for mutual understanding. When people share their true motives and fears, they invite others to join in the decision-making process. This kind of openness fosters a sense of belonging and reinforces the idea that everyone is working toward a common goal. Picture a team tackling a tough project. If every member shares their concerns and hopes openly, they can coordinate their efforts more effectively, creating an environment where cooperation thrives.

Let's take a look at a nonprofit organization striving for a worthy cause. When the leadership clearly communicates their vision and involves team members in decision-making, trust naturally develops. Volunteers who feel appreciated and included are more likely to give their all, leading to a stronger commitment to the mission. This shared sense of purpose transforms what might have been a solo effort into a collective journey, where every member feels equally invested in the outcome.

Transparency not only fosters trust but also promotes accountability. When people make their intentions known, they hold themselves and each other accountable for their actions. This accountability acts like a safety net, discouraging self-serving behaviors that could endanger the group. If everyone acknowledges their roles in a shared project, they create a culture where straying from the agreed path is less likely to happen. This sense of responsibility reinforces cooperation, making it easier for individuals to contribute positively.

Another effective strategy to promote cooperation is encouraging communication. Keeping the lines of dialogue open can help bridge the gaps that often lead to misunderstandings and resentment. When people talk about their thoughts, feelings, and concerns, they break down the myths of isolation that the Prisoner's Dilemma can create. In the workplace, regular check-ins and feedback sessions help teams stay on the same page, reducing the chance of miscommunication that could lead to betrayal. The simple act of sharing ideas can turn a potentially adversarial situation into a collaborative problem-solving session.

Let's think about the healthcare sector, where cooperation is crucial. In hospitals, creating a culture of communication can be transformative. When medical staff share information about a patient's condition, treatment options, and possible outcomes, they reduce the chances of errors and enhance the quality of care. This teamwork not only benefits patients but also strengthens relationships among team members, creating a united front that can tackle challenges more effectively.

However, communication should be more than just one-sided; it needs to encourage active listening. When individuals express their thoughts and genuinely consider others' views, they develop empathy—a key ingredient for successful cooperation. Empathy allows us to look beyond our own needs and understand the hopes and fears of those around us. This understanding can change how we make decisions, leading to solutions that benefit everyone, not just a select few.

Besides trust and communication, the frequency of interactions also plays a crucial role in fostering cooperation. When we engage with others repeatedly, it creates familiarity, which can lessen the perceived risks of collaboration. The more we interact, the better we understand each other's intentions and behaviors. This comfort helps us feel more secure in our choices to cooperate.

Think about a classic example from sports. Team dynamics often rely on repeated interactions. Players who practice together regularly build a strong sense of trust and friendship. They learn to anticipate each other's moves on the field, which translates into better teamwork during games. As they work together more often, their ability to cooperate under pressure improves, leading to better performance and shared victories. The takeaways from these environments emphasize the importance of investing time in building relationships that reach beyond immediate situations.

Moreover, reputation plays a significant role too. When individuals or groups anticipate future interactions, they often consider the long-term outcomes of their actions. This awareness, known as the "shadow of the future," encourages cooperation. When people realize that their choices today will shape how they are viewed in future interactions, they are more inclined to act in ways that support collaboration.

Take online communities as an example. In platforms where users continually engage with one another, reputation systems often develop. Users earn points or ratings based on their contributions and behavior. Those who consistently engage in cooperative actions tend to build a positive reputation, which becomes a valuable asset in future interactions. The fear of harming their reputation can discourage selfish behavior, fostering a self-regulating environment where cooperation flourishes.

In personal relationships, reciprocity is another critical factor in overcoming the dilemma. When individuals perform acts of kindness or support, they create a cycle of goodwill that encourages further cooperation. This cycle builds momentum, as one kind act often inspires another. Whether it's offering help to a friend or making compromises in a romantic relationship, these small gestures lay the foundation for a strong, mutually supportive bond.

To illustrate, think about a neighborly relationship. When one neighbor mows the lawn for an elderly resident, that act of kindness doesn't go unnoticed; it often leads to a reciprocal gesture. The elderly neighbor might bake cookies or take care of the neighbor's pets in return. This cycle of goodwill not only strengthens their bond but also nurtures a sense of community, where people see the value of cooperation over competition.

In the arena of public policy, the challenge of cooperation can seem daunting, but it's not impossible. Policymakers face this dilemma when crafting policies that require collective action, like public health initiatives or infrastructure development. Here, fostering collaboration and mutual support can be achieved through incentives. Governments can create programs that reward individuals and organizations for working together, such as grants for community projects or recognition for businesses embracing sustainable practices.

For example, consider a community initiative aimed at revamping local parks. If local authorities provide funding for groups that join forces to clean up and beautify park spaces, it encourages participation and fosters a shared sense of pride. This incentive breaks down the walls of self-interest, leading to a united vision of community improvement that benefits everyone. As individuals see the tangible results of their collaboration, the cycle of teamwork continues, reinforcing the importance of working together.

Education systems also play a vital role in developing cooperative skills. Teaching children about the importance of collaboration from an early age helps instill values they will carry into adulthood. Programs that focus on group projects, peer mediation, and conflict resolution allow students to practice cooperative behavior in a safe environment. As they learn to tackle challenges together, they become skilled at recognizing the benefits of cooperation throughout their lives.

The value of empathy and understanding others' perspectives cannot be overstated in this context. Kids who are taught to appreciate the feelings and viewpoints of others are more likely to embrace collaborative approaches as they grow. Encouraging open discussions about emotions and experiences in classrooms builds emotional intelligence, leading to a generation that prioritizes cooperation over competition.

Finally, we must acknowledge the role of leadership in promoting cooperation. Effective leaders can set the tone for a culture that values collaboration. Leaders who exemplify cooperative behavior, promote open communication, and actively build trust create an environment where people feel empowered to work together.

Imagine a company led by a CEO who champions teamwork and collaboration. By openly discussing successes and failures, the leader fosters a culture of accountability and trust. Employees are more likely to engage in cooperative behaviors, knowing their contributions matter. A visionary leader can inspire collective action, transforming the workplace into a vibrant ecosystem of collaboration.

The strategies to tackle the challenges posed by the Prisoner's Dilemma are within our reach, but they require dedication and effort. By prioritizing trust, encouraging communication, embracing repeated interactions, promoting reciprocity, offering incentives for cooperation, and nurturing effective leadership, we can create an environment ripe for collaboration.

Chapter 3: Zero-Sum and Non-Zero-Sum Games—Winning Together or Alone

Defining the Stakes

At its heart, game theory offers a captivating look into how people and groups interact, make choices, and strategize through various situations. Two of the most important ideas in this field are zero-sum and non-zero-sum games. Simply put, these concepts show how gains and losses are shared among participants in any scenario. Grasping these differences is vital, not just for game theory experts but for anyone looking to navigate the tricky waters of human interaction—whether that's in business, personal relationships, or everyday life.

Let's start with zero-sum games. Imagine a situation where the stakes are very clear: for every gain one person makes, another suffers an equal loss. This idea is easy to grasp with familiar examples. Think about a poker game, where the pot is the total money in play. Each dollar one player wins means a dollar lost by someone else. At the end of the game, the total of everyone's winnings and losses adds up to zero. This perfectly captures the essence of a zero-sum game: when one player wins, another must lose, and the overall amount of "wealth" stays the same.

Zero-sum games often bring to mind cutthroat competition. In the business world, this can show up when companies fight for the same customers or market share. If one business grabs a bigger piece of the pie, it leaves less for its competitors. This creates a mindset of scarcity, where it seems that for one company to succeed, others have to fail. It's a tough reality that can lead to aggressive tactics, which hurt trust and teamwork.

Consider a typical workplace where everyone is competing for promotions or bonuses. This zero-sum mentality can create a toxic environment, turning coworkers into rivals, all believing that only one can win. This not only harms relationships but also holds back creativity and teamwork. Employees might keep helpful information to themselves, afraid that sharing it could hurt their chances of getting ahead.

But zero-sum thinking isn't just a business issue; it seeps into our daily lives, creating unnecessary stress in our personal relationships. Picture a family game night where siblings fiercely compete in board games or video games. The excitement of winning often gets overshadowed by the pain of losing, leading to arguments and rivalries that can last long after the games end.

Now, let's shift gears and look at non-zero-sum games, which offer a brighter, more cooperative view. Non-zero-sum games happen when the total gains and losses among participants don't have to cancel each other out. In these situations, it's quite possible for everyone involved to benefit or suffer together, creating lots of chances for teamwork and shared success.

For example, think about a strong business partnership. Picture two companies teaming up to work on a joint project, combining their resources and skills to create something greater than either could have done alone. By joining forces, they not only boost their chances of success but also expand the market, opening up new opportunities that help both companies thrive. This win-win situation captures the spirit of non-zero-sum thinking, where working together sparks growth and innovation.

Similarly, consider community projects aimed at enhancing local life. When neighbors come together to create a community garden, they're doing more than just sharing a piece of land; they're building connections. Each person gets fresh produce, but they also enjoy friendships and a strengthened sense of community. These benefits can't be measured in simple gains and losses; they reflect a rich collection of shared moments and growth.

To clarify these ideas even more, visual aids can be really helpful. Diagrams showing the clear differences between zero-sum and non-zero-sum games can make it easier to understand what's going on. For instance, a graph might illustrate how resources stay fixed in a zero-sum game, compared to the expanding potential in a non-zero-sum situation, giving us clear insights into how different mindsets can shape outcomes.

Real-life stories can also deepen our understanding of these theories. Imagine two neighboring businesses competing for customers. One business adopts a zero-sum mindset, seeing every customer as a lost opportunity for its rival. The other business, however, takes a non-zero-sum approach, realizing that working together—like through referrals or joint promotions—can enhance the overall attractiveness of the area, bringing more customers to both. In this case, both businesses can thrive, showing that cooperation often leads to better outcomes than fierce competition.

By being aware of these two types of games, we can start to rethink how we engage with others. It's crucial to look at our lives for instances where we might be stuck in a zero-sum mindset, affecting our choices and relationships. Shifting towards a non-zero-sum perspective can open the door to collaboration, innovation, and harmony, ultimately leading to more rewarding experiences.

In the context of neighborly relations, consider the dynamics that often arise. A disagreement over property lines can escalate into a bitter feud driven by a zero-sum mindset. However, when both sides choose to communicate and seek common ground—maybe by agreeing on a shared fence or starting a community garden—they can transform a tense situation into a partnership. These kinds of changes highlight how seeing others as potential allies instead of competitors can lead to positive outcomes.

As we go through life, being aware of whether we're thinking in zero-sum or non-zero-sum terms can greatly affect how we interact with others. This awareness influences our decisions and shapes the quality of our relationships and the happiness we find in them. It encourages us to think about how we can create environments that promote teamwork, creativity, and support instead of rivalry and conflict.

Adopting the principles of non-zero-sum games can spark meaningful changes in how we handle different aspects of our lives. The challenge is recognizing when we slip into a zero-sum mindset and working to change our perspective. This shift may involve reassessing our goals, changing how we communicate, and looking for collaboration opportunities, even in competitive environments.

Ultimately, understanding the stakes involved in zero-sum and non-zero-sum games gives us valuable tools for navigating our personal and professional lives. By realizing that competition and cooperation can coexist, we can find paths that lead to shared success and fulfillment. This journey starts with a simple change in how we see things: a willingness to embrace collaboration as a rewarding choice in a world that often focuses on competition.

Applications in Negotiation

Negotiation is like a dance—a careful balancing act that challenges us to stand up for ourselves while also understanding what others need. It's this back-and-forth that shows us just how game theory can shape our conversations and agreements. By looking at negotiation tactics through the ideas of zero-sum and non-zero-sum games, we can gather insights that not only improve our strategies but also make our outcomes more meaningful.

In many negotiations, people often fall into a zero-sum way of thinking. This is especially common when parties see the stakes as fixed, believing that if one person gains something, the other loses an equal amount. Take salary negotiations, for example: when an employee successfully asks for a raise, it might feel like the employer is losing that money, creating a story where one person's win becomes another's loss. This zero-sum mindset can push negotiators to adopt more aggressive approaches, thinking they have to fight to come out ahead.

Imagine an employee who approaches their manager, feeling confident about their work, and asks for a salary bump. The manager, however, views the budget as a zero-sum game. If they agree to the raise, they might feel they're robbing funds that could be used for promotions or bonuses for other team members. This mindset can lead the manager to become defensive, justifying why the employee doesn't deserve a raise instead of having an open conversation about their contributions and potential.

In these situations, it's important for negotiators to spot the zero-sum dynamics at play. Once they do, they can start to change their approach. Instead of treating the conversation like a battle, they can shift to a broader view of negotiation. For example, the employee might focus on how their work adds value to the company rather than just pushing for personal gain. By showing how their contributions help the team or organization succeed, they can change the discussion from one of lack to one of opportunity—where investing in the employee could actually benefit the company.

Moving from a zero-sum mindset to a non-zero-sum perspective can really change the game in negotiations. In a non-zero-sum negotiation, both sides can find ways to benefit. This is especially powerful when parties share common interests or goals. The trick is to spot these shared interests and find common ground where everyone feels like they've gained something.

Consider a negotiation between two companies looking to form a partnership. If they see this as a zero-sum game, they will likely each try to negotiate the best terms for themselves, risking a partnership full of disagreements. However, if they can recognize the potential for a non-zero-sum outcome, they can brainstorm ways to create a win-win situation.

This shift requires changing how they think, moving from a competitive attitude to one of teamwork. The companies might engage in integrative bargaining, where they collaborate to understand their mutual interests and explore creative solutions that benefit everyone. For instance, they could come up with ways to combine their resources, cutting costs while improving their products to attract more customers. This cooperative approach often leads to stronger relationships built on trust and shared success, laying the groundwork for further collaboration in the future.

Real-life examples show how non-zero-sum strategies can lead to successful negotiations. A great case is the merger of two tech giants, where both companies realized that combining their strengths could lead to a powerful partnership far greater than what either could achieve alone. Instead of getting stuck arguing over how to divide resources or equity, they focused on aligning their visions for innovation and customer satisfaction. The result? A smooth merger that not only benefited shareholders but also led to groundbreaking advances in technology that neither could have accomplished alone.

Another strong example can be seen in peace negotiations between countries. When conflicting parties sit down with a zero-sum mindset, the chances of reaching a lasting agreement drop significantly. But when negotiators prioritize understanding everyone's underlying needs, they can find solutions that address those needs. A successful peace treaty often includes elements that allow all sides to feel like they've gained something valuable, whether it's security, economic benefits, or cultural recognition.

To make the most of non-zero-sum negotiation strategies, individuals can adopt several practical tactics. Active listening is key; truly hearing and understanding the other party's concerns and interests helps negotiators find common ground that may not be immediately obvious. This requires setting aside one's own agenda for a moment and genuinely engaging with the other side.

Additionally, brainstorming sessions can work wonders in uncovering creative solutions. By creating an environment where everyone can propose ideas without fear of criticism, negotiators often stumble upon innovative compromises that benefit both sides. This collaborative atmosphere fosters a sense of investment in the process, empowering everyone to work together toward a shared goal.

So, exploring how game theory applies to negotiation reveals various paths we can take when facing conflicts and choices. Whether we find ourselves in a boardroom, at a community meeting, or having a simple chat with a friend, understanding the concepts of zero-sum and non-zero-sum games can help guide us toward more productive interactions.

Preparation is also vital. Entering negotiations with a clear grasp of your own needs and interests is crucial, but it's just as important to anticipate what the other party might need. This holistic view helps negotiators uncover collaborative solutions that benefit everyone involved.

Ultimately, negotiation isn't just about winning; it's about creating agreements that lift everyone up. Embracing a non-zero-sum mindset can lead to a more fulfilling experience, allowing individuals to build relationships based on trust and mutual benefit.

As we navigate the complex world of negotiations in both our personal and professional lives, let's keep in mind that the best outcomes often come from valuing collaboration over competition. By rethinking our negotiations through the lens of game theory, we can discover strategies that respect the interests of everyone involved. Whether we're aiming for a raise, forming a partnership, or resolving a conflict, the principles of non-zero-sum negotiation can help us achieve outcomes that leave everyone feeling valued and understood.

In the rich landscape of human interaction, mastering negotiation can transform not just the results of our discussions but the very quality of our relationships. By embracing the insights of game theory, we can work towards a future where cooperation takes center stage, allowing us to thrive together in a world full of possibilities for shared success.

Creating Win-Win Situations

When we think about success, the saying "a rising tide lifts all boats" really hits home. It reminds us that working together can create benefits for everyone involved. This idea isn't just a nice thought; it's something we can use every day in our lives. Whether we're chatting with friends, collaborating with coworkers, or engaging in our communities, making win-win situations is all about shifting our mindset to focus on cooperation, understanding, and open conversations. Each of us can help create an atmosphere where everyone feels appreciated and heard, breaking free from the competition that often holds us back.

At the core of this change is the idea of collaboration. When we adopt a collaborative mindset, we start to view our interactions as opportunities to work together rather than compete against one another. This shift in thinking helps us connect with others as partners instead of rivals. By prioritizing clear communication and really listening to each other, we can discover shared goals and dreams, which are essential for successful teamwork.

Picture a situation at work where a team is racing against a tight deadline. Instead of viewing each other as rivals fighting for the spotlight, what if they treated it as a group effort? By talking openly about their obstacles and genuinely listening to one another, they can pinpoint each team member's strengths and areas for growth. Maybe one person shines in project management while another has a talent for creative solutions. By appreciating each other's unique skills and teaming up, they can create a plan that not only meets the deadline but surpasses expectations. This example shows how a win-win mindset can turn a tense moment into a chance for everyone to succeed together.

Empathy is a key part of building these collaborative spaces. It's about understanding where someone else is coming from and what they need. When we practice empathy, we open ourselves up to discovering shared interests where everyone can benefit. For instance, in negotiations, if we focus only on our own needs, we might miss out on solutions that could work for both sides. When both parties feel valued and understood, they're far more likely to support each other's success, leading to trust and goodwill.

To nurture a win-win mindset, we need to be open to finding common goals. In any interaction—be it a business collaboration or a community project—spotting shared objectives can set the stage for teamwork. Consider two companies thinking about merging. At first, they might both be focused on competing for the best deal. However, if they shift their view to highlight their mutual goals—like reaching more customers, enhancing satisfaction, or driving innovation—they can come up with a plan that boosts the strengths of both. This cooperative approach not only reduces tension but also builds a stronger partnership with a clear path to achievement.

Moving towards a mindset where everyone can benefit is crucial for creating these win-win scenarios. Unlike situations where one person's gain means another's loss, non-zero-sum situations allow for multiple winners. This is especially true in community efforts, where teamwork can lead to solutions that uplift entire neighborhoods. Imagine a community facing high unemployment. Local businesses, schools, and government agencies can come together to develop job training programs. By combining their resources and knowledge, they can create opportunities for people to gain valuable skills, making the workforce stronger while uplifting the community as a whole. This shared commitment results in a cycle of success, showing that working together often brings better results than competing against each other.

Real-world examples highlight the success of creating win-win situations. One well-known case is the partnership between Starbucks and Conservation International. When facing the challenge of sourcing coffee sustainably, Starbucks realized that its success depended on the health of coffee-growing regions. By teaming up with Conservation International, they launched a program aimed at promoting sustainable farming among coffee producers. This initiative ensured a reliable supply of high-quality coffee for Starbucks while also helping farmers improve their livelihoods through training and resources. The outcome? A thriving coffee industry that benefits both the company and the communities involved.

Another example can be found in environmental efforts. Picture a group of manufacturers joining forces to lower their carbon footprint. Instead of each company trying to outshine the others with separate projects, they could collaborate to share ideas and resources. By working together on eco-friendly technology, they can cut costs and speed up their progress toward sustainability goals. This shared approach not only enhances each company's reputation but also contributes to a broader shift towards environmental responsibility.

The importance of collaborative strategies becomes even clearer in the realm of negotiation. When we approach discussions with the goal of creating win-win solutions, we foster a spirit of teamwork that can lead to groundbreaking agreements. For example, in labor negotiations, unions and employers often find themselves at odds, each advocating for very different interests. However, when both sides come together to explore common goals—like workplace safety, employee satisfaction, and productivity—they can co-create agreements that benefit everyone involved. This method not only resolves immediate issues but also lays the groundwork for future teamwork and communication, strengthening their relationship.

As we think about the power of creating win-win situations, it's crucial to recognize practical strategies we can implement. To truly nurture a collaborative atmosphere, we can adopt several useful tactics. First, open communication is key. By promoting honest conversations and transparency, we can create a space where everyone feels safe to share their thoughts and concerns. This openness allows us to explore options we may not have considered before.

Active listening is another vital aspect. It means not just hearing the words spoken but also grasping the feelings and motivations behind them. By acknowledging others' viewpoints, we build trust and rapport—both of which are essential for effective collaboration.

Moreover, brainstorming sessions can be a great way to spark innovative ideas. In a friendly and open atmosphere where all suggestions are welcome, participants can think creatively and propose solutions that lead to win-win outcomes. This team brainstorming not only encourages participation but also fosters a sense of ownership and commitment to the ideas generated.

Additionally, regularly reflecting on our teamwork efforts can help us identify areas we can improve. By looking back at what worked well and what didn't, we can refine our approach over time. This dedication to getting better will help us become more effective collaborators, leading to even greater successes in our interactions.

As we navigate life's complexities, let's embrace cooperation over competition. By understanding that our successes can be intertwined, we open ourselves up to a world where everyone can win. Whether in our personal lives, professional endeavors, or community projects, the willingness to build collaborative relationships can lead to amazing results.

The message is clear: look for opportunities to collaborate in your own life. Whether at work, at home, or in your neighborhood, seek ways to create win-win scenarios. Find common goals and invite others into conversations that emphasize open communication and empathy. Together, we can cultivate a rich environment of shared success, where cooperation is at the forefront and everyone's interests are uplifted.

Ultimately, the journey to creating win-win situations is more than just about personal gain; it's about embracing the power of collaboration and recognizing the incredible potential we have when we work together. As we foster this mindset, we'll become better equipped to handle the challenges life brings us, leading to more meaningful relationships and impactful outcomes. The world is brimming with opportunities waiting for us to explore; let's grab them together and create a future where cooperation and shared success shine bright.

Chapter 4: Nash Equilibrium—Finding Balance Among Competing Interests

Equilibrium Explained

In the world of strategic interactions, where our choices often depend on what others do, the idea of Nash Equilibrium shines as a valuable tool for understanding. Named after the brilliant mathematician John Nash, this concept is based on a straightforward yet powerful idea: each person in a game picks their best strategy, considering what others have chosen. When everyone finds their equilibrium, no one can do better by changing their strategy alone. It's a careful interplay of cooperation and competition, where every move matters, the stakes are high, and the results can be quite surprising.

To bring this idea to life, let's think about a relatable example: two friends, Alex and Jamie, who have decided to go out for dinner together. They're both eager to try something new, and the popular choices are a trendy Italian restaurant and a talked-about sushi bar. The tricky part? Their tastes are somewhat similar, but there's a catch. If they both pick the same restaurant, they might end up waiting forever for a table. However, if they go their separate ways, one might end up eating alone at a less appealing place.

At this point, their decision-making process feels like a strategic game. Alex loves sushi, while Jamie has a soft spot for pasta. Each one has to think about what the other might choose. If Alex thinks Jamie will go for sushi, he might decide to join her, but the fear of long wait times might push him toward the Italian spot instead. On the flip side, Jamie is in the same boat. If they both believe they'll end up at the same place, their plans could quickly turn into a frustrating experience.

We can break down this scenario mathematically, with the strategies looking like this:

- If both choose the Italian restaurant, they'll be satisfied but might face a long wait.
- If one picks sushi and the other Italian, the one dining alone may feel a pang of regret, wondering what they could have enjoyed.
- If they both choose different restaurants, they might have decent meals but could find themselves

wishing they'd chosen the other's favorite.

In this situation, the Nash Equilibrium happens when both friends choose the restaurant that brings them the most satisfaction based on their guesses about each other's decisions. For example, if they both pick sushi but find the place packed, they might feel disappointed. On the other hand, if one picks Italian while the other confidently chooses sushi, they both get to enjoy their favorites, though they might still wonder about the meal they didn't share.

This simple dinner dilemma shows us the main idea behind Nash Equilibrium: understanding and predicting what others will do can lead to better outcomes. This idea really captures the essence of strategic interactions in our daily lives. From sharing a meal to making business deals, the principles of Nash Equilibrium can be found in nearly every decision-making setting.

Beyond dinner plans, this equilibrium plays a vital role in many areas of life, including shopping habits, social situations, and even global economics. Imagine yourself in a busy market, surrounded by vendors selling their goods. As you navigate through the hustle and bustle, your choices about what to buy are influenced not just by what you want, but also by what other shoppers are doing. If you see a crowd gathering around a certain stall, you might feel drawn to that product, even if it wasn't on your list.

Retailers experience this dynamic as well. They're always watching their competitors, changing their prices and promotions to grab the attention of shoppers. If one store lowers its prices, it might attract a flock of customers, but if other stores do the same, the balance shifts again. Here, Nash Equilibrium shows up as a balancing act between what's available and what people want, where businesses must think not only about their own strategies but also how their rivals will respond.

Grasping the implications of Nash Equilibrium isn't just an academic exercise; it's a crucial skill for navigating the twists and turns of human interaction. Success in both personal and professional settings often relies on understanding where everyone stands and how they might react to different actions.

There's a theoretical foundation to this equilibrium, which is rooted in math but is still easy to understand. For a Nash Equilibrium to happen, a few conditions need to be in place. The strategies available to everyone must be clear, and they need to have sensible reasons for their choices. This doesn't mean every player will always do what's best for themselves—people can be unpredictable—but it does assume they'll consistently pick strategies that they believe will lead to the best possible outcomes, based on their expectations of what others will do.

To clarify this idea further, let's look at a classic example in game theory: the Prisoner's Dilemma. Here, two suspects are arrested and questioned separately. Each has the choice to either stick together by remaining silent or betray the other by confessing. If both stay quiet, they'll get a light sentence. If one betrays while the other stays silent, the betrayer walks free, and the silent partner faces the worst punishment. If they both betray each other, they end up with moderate sentences. The equilibrium occurs when both decide to betray, as it's the only choice that ensures they won't end up worse off than if they had cooperated.

This shows that while working together might bring about the best result for both, individual reasoning often leads both parties toward a less favorable outcome. These sorts of scenarios pop up all the time in our lives—every time you decide whether to trust someone or look out for your own interests, you're navigating the complexities of Nash Equilibrium.

Recognizing Nash Equilibrium helps people enhance their decision-making, whether they're negotiating a deal, leading a team, or just trying to satisfy their cravings at dinner. It encourages a way of thinking that anticipates what others might do, promotes strategic thinking, and fosters awareness of the delicate balance between working together and competing.

By understanding the heart of equilibrium, individuals can make smarter choices that lead to better outcomes—not just for themselves, but for those around them too. Whether in business, relationships, or daily interactions, realizing the significance of strategic thinking can turn regular situations into chances for mutual gain.

So, the next time you find yourself faced with a decision that could be influenced by others—whether you're picking a restaurant, negotiating a deal, or even choosing a spot on a crowded bus—take a moment to reflect on the ideas of Nash Equilibrium. Your choices might create a ripple effect that reaches further than you think, highlighting the intricate web of connections that link us all in our search for balance amid competing interests.

Strategic Stability

In the world of competition, where every choice is linked to the decisions of others, understanding strategic stability is crucial. As we explore the twists and turns of markets and social environments, learning why certain balances hold steady can give us great insight into how individuals, companies, and entire communities behave. This kind of stability helps different players find their place in a world that's always changing, leading to results that might seem surprising but make perfect sense strategically.

Take the smartphone industry, for example. It's a high-stakes battleground where companies like Apple and Samsung engage in a careful dance, always adjusting to each other's moves. Decisions about pricing, product launches, and marketing campaigns are all part of a delicate balance where each player must consider what their competitors might do. When Apple unveils a new iPhone, Samsung doesn't just sit back; it jumps into action, tweaking its own strategies on the fly. This balance isn't just a brief pause but a vibrant state influenced by shifts in consumer tastes, tech advancements, and competitive tactics.

Think about the massive effort that goes into planning an iPhone launch. Apple has to think not only about what customers will want but also how Samsung will respond. If Apple decides to lower prices, Samsung might feel pressured to do the same or risk losing customers. On the flip side, if Samsung rolls out an exciting new feature, Apple could rush to innovate so it doesn't seem left behind. This constant back-and-forth creates a strategic stability where both companies are in a state of mutual influence, with each strategy finely tuned to react to the other's actions.

Looking closer at this scenario, we can see that strategic stability is built on the expectations each company has about the other. If both believe sticking to their current strategies will lead to good results, they are likely to keep doing what they're doing. If one company changes course, it disrupts the balance, forcing reactions that could lead to a new, though temporary, state of equilibrium. This often plays out in price wars, where companies fight back against each other's pricing strategies, causing profits to drop for everyone involved. It might look like one company is gaining an advantage, but really, the situation remains fluid, with each move provoking a response.

Now, let's step away from technology and think about the social structures that shape our everyday lives. The idea of Nash Equilibrium often comes into play here, influencing behaviors that become instinctive. Picture your morning drive; the unwritten rule of driving on a certain side of the road illustrates how everyone sticking to the same practice leads to stability. Each driver's decision to follow this norm depends on the belief that others will do the same. If one driver chooses to break from this convention, the potential chaos that follows shows just how fragile that balance can be.

These unspoken guidelines affect not just driving habits but also countless social interactions. For instance, consider the clothes you pick for a formal event. The expectation that guests will wear business or formal attire creates a setting where everyone feels comfortable following these social norms. If someone shows up in casual clothes, they disrupt the balance and might face social awkwardness or exclusion. This shared commitment to social conventions demonstrates how people navigate their choices, balancing personal style with the desire to blend in.

The foundation of this strategic stability often rests on the idea of mutual assurance. In many situations, people watch each other's behavior to make smart choices. If everyone at an event opts for formal attire, it strengthens the idea that this is the norm, making others reconsider any casual plans in favor of fitting in. This collective behavior creates a cycle where the balance is upheld through shared expectations and actions.

So, how can you use the concept of strategic stability in your own life? Understanding Nash Equilibrium can help you make better decisions in many situations, whether at work, in negotiations, or within family matters. To navigate these complexities effectively, it's important to recognize the roles each person plays, along with their goals and strategies.

In the workplace, for instance, understanding team dynamics often requires paying attention to the balance that exists among coworkers. If one person consistently takes on more tasks, it could lead to an imbalance that makes others react, either positively or negatively. People observing this might feel they need to step up to restore balance or choose to remain passive, which could lead to resentment or exhaustion. By creating an environment where roles and expectations are clear, teams can achieve a kind of strategic stability that supports teamwork and productivity.

Negotiations also provide a chance to tap into strategic stability. Before entering discussions, it's key to think about the other party's perspectives and objectives. By predicting how they might respond to different proposals, you can develop a strategy that aims not only for your own goals but also respects the interests of everyone involved. This kind of foresight can lead to agreements that benefit both sides, reinforcing a sense of balance.

Family decisions often reflect similar dynamics, where being willing to understand and accommodate everyone's preferences can lead to smoother interactions. Whether you're deciding on where to go for a vacation or what to do on the weekend, recognizing the value of group input helps keep things harmonious and fosters unity. By aligning individual wishes with the family's expectations, decisions can be made more easily, resulting in outcomes that work for everyone.

In short, strategic stability is about seeing the complex web of interactions that shape our choices and behaviors. It encourages a mindset that values cooperation and foresight, while also recognizing the competitive elements that can arise. By sharpening your ability to see the balance that exists in different situations, you can make more thoughtful decisions that benefit not just yourself but also those around you.

As you go about your daily life, think about how strategic stability plays a role in your interactions. Whether you're working with colleagues, hanging out with friends, or navigating family dynamics, the principles of Nash Equilibrium are likely at work in ways you might not even notice. By deepening your understanding of these dynamics, you can strengthen your decision-making skills, leading to outcomes that promote harmony and cooperation amid the competing interests we all face in our shared experiences.

With each decision, remember that the delicate balance of our interactions is a dance of strategy and expectation. Embracing this complexity can turn everyday moments into chances for growth, connection, and mutual benefit as we navigate the intricate landscape of human relationships and the decisions that shape our lives.

Case Studies

Grasping the idea of Nash Equilibrium can feel a bit like trying to catch a butterfly—it's beautiful, complex, and sometimes hard to pin down. But if we take a moment to observe how it flutters about, we can start to see the patterns and principles at play. To make these concepts easier to understand, let's look at some real-life examples that illustrate Nash Equilibrium in action. By diving into history, business situations, and public policy decisions, we'll uncover how strategic choices unfold in everyday life.

One of the most striking examples of Nash Equilibrium comes from the Cold War, a time filled with tension, fear, and the constant threat of nuclear destruction. During this era, the idea of deterrence emerged as a guiding force for the superpowers. It was based on the understanding that any act of aggression would lead to a devastating counterattack. In this scenario, equilibrium was reached through the grim reality of mutual assured destruction—both sides had enough nuclear weapons to ensure that any attack would lead to catastrophic consequences for everyone involved.

In this high-stakes situation, neither the United States nor the Soviet Union wanted to start a conflict. The choices they made were based on the belief that the other side would avoid escalating tensions, thus keeping a fragile peace. This balance didn't stem from trust but rather from the chilling recognition that neither could win in a nuclear war. Each superpower worked to maintain its arsenal while avoiding actions that might provoke the other.

A key moment that tested this delicate balance was the Cuban Missile Crisis. When the U.S. discovered Soviet missiles in Cuba, the world held its breath. A potential showdown loomed, but both leaders—U.S. President John F. Kennedy and Soviet Premier Nikita Khrushchev—understood the weight of making a wrong move. In this tense standoff, both sides took steps to back away from disaster, ultimately finding a resolution that highlighted the power of strategic thinking. The agreement to remove the missiles from both countries illustrates how a grasp of Nash Equilibrium can help leaders navigate dangerous waters by anticipating how their adversaries will react.

Now, let's shift from global politics to the business world, where Nash Equilibrium plays a crucial role in competitive industries. Take the airline industry, for example. Here, companies constantly tweak their pricing and route strategies based on what their competitors do. If one airline drops its fares on a popular route, others feel pressured to follow suit, often leading to a fierce pricing battle.

What often happens is that the airlines reach a Nash Equilibrium, where they settle into a pricing pattern that takes into account their own costs and their competitors' prices. You can see this equilibrium in the steadiness of ticket prices for similar routes across different airlines, as each company weighs the chance of losing customers against the risks of undercutting their competition. In this case, the stability arises because airlines need to balance their desire to make a profit with the need to stay competitive.

Even decisions about launching new routes or services are influenced by this equilibrium. For instance, if an airline is considering entering a new market, it has to think about whether its rivals will jump in too. If one airline believes that another might offer competitive fares, it may decide not to enter the market at all, thus preserving the status quo. This strategic dance among airlines shows how Nash Equilibrium shapes pricing strategies and decisions about growth and service offerings.

Now, let's step into the world of public policy, where the ideas behind Nash Equilibrium also resonate, especially in environmental agreements. A notable example is the Paris Agreement, where countries around the world come together to tackle climate change. The challenge is finding a balance between each nation's interests and the shared commitment to cut carbon emissions.

In these complicated negotiations, countries have to consider their own goals while predicting what others will do. Each nation faces the tough choice of whether to commit to ambitious targets or prioritize its economic growth. The equilibrium here is often shaky, as countries weigh the advantages of working together against the risk of free-riding—where some countries benefit from the efforts of others without doing their part.

The Paris Agreement is a significant milestone, showing that countries can find common ground, but the risk remains. If too many countries don't meet their commitments, the agreement could fall apart, leading to less cooperation. Here, Nash Equilibrium shines through as countries strive to align their national interests with the global need for a sustainable future.

Moreover, public policy on climate change shows how Nash Equilibrium extends beyond international agreements to local initiatives. Imagine a city trying to roll out a recycling program. The success of this program depends on residents' willingness to participate; however, if a large number of people choose not to recycle, the whole initiative could fail. In this case, the equilibrium relies on everyone coming together, with each person's choice influenced by their neighbors' behavior. If people believe that those around them will recycle, they're more likely to join in, creating a positive cycle of cooperation.

As we reflect on these case studies, it's clear that Nash Equilibrium operates in many different contexts. The skill of anticipating others' choices while making decisions is essential in various situations. Whether in the tense atmosphere of the Cold War, the competitive world of airlines, or the collaborative fight against climate change, understanding this equilibrium can guide decision-making in numerous ways.

Think about how the principles of Nash Equilibrium might apply in your own life. Every interaction—whether at work, at home, or in social settings—offers opportunities for strategic decision-making. Understanding how our choices influence one another can help you navigate challenges more effectively.

Imagine a scenario at work where several team members are competing for the same promotion. Each person needs to consider their own ambitions alongside how others are perceived. By understanding the balance at play, team members can adjust their approaches, perhaps by collaborating more closely or developing unique skills that make them stand out. The dynamics within the team can significantly influence individual outcomes, revealing paths to success that may not have been obvious at first.

Similarly, in family life, decisions often reflect an equilibrium shaped by shared expectations. Think about planning a family vacation; the preferences of each member have to be considered, and finding common ground fosters a sense of togetherness. By being aware of others' perspectives and adjusting your plans accordingly, you can create enjoyable experiences for everyone, strengthening the family bond.

Navigating the complexities of human relationships—whether at work or in personal life—requires a good grasp of the principles of Nash Equilibrium. Reflecting on your own experiences can help you realize how the choices you make can lead to outcomes that benefit not just you, but those around you, too.

The dance of strategy and expectation occurs in our daily lives, often in subtle yet significant ways. By developing a clearer understanding of these dynamics, you empower yourself to make choices that contribute to a more harmonious environment. Embrace the complexities of human interaction, and recognize the opportunities for growth and connection that lie within strategic thinking.

Understanding the nuances of Nash Equilibrium lets you view the world through a more analytical lens. Whether you find yourself in competition or collaboration, the lessons from these case studies can guide you. As you move forward, remember that the delicate balance of interactions isn't just a theoretical idea—it's a lived experience filled with chances for success and personal development.

Chapter 5: Coordination Games—Achieving Harmony

The Battle of Perspectives

Picture yourself in a lively café, where the scent of freshly brewed coffee dances in the air alongside the laughter and chatter of those around you. A group of friends is gathered at a table, eagerly sharing their plans for the weekend. One friend suggests a hiking trip, another proposes a cozy movie night, and yet another throws out the idea of a spontaneous road trip. Each person presents their own vision for a perfect weekend, and before long, the playful debate begins—everyone wants to have a say, but they struggle to find common ground. What could be a simple decision turns into a mini-dance of opinions, personal preferences, and subtle hints. This lively exchange is more than just casual talk about how to spend their days off; it represents a coordination game—a situation where people need to align their choices to reach an outcome that everyone is happy with.

Coordination games are intriguing because they highlight how important it is to share an understanding. Unlike competitive games, where one person's win means another's loss, coordination games thrive on working together. Here, the aim isn't to outsmart each other but to seek a common solution. Teamwork becomes the secret ingredient for success, as agreeing on a plan can lead to a win-win situation. But the trick is navigating the different perspectives at play. How do you find the best option when everyone sees things differently?

Often, the answer lies in our psychology—the complex mental processes that shape our decisions. The café scene shows just how differing viewpoints can lead to confusion and indecision. Each friend has a unique picture of what their ideal weekend looks like, and without a common thread to bring their ideas together, they risk having no plan at all. This is where the idea of focal points comes into play, acting as a guiding light amid the sea of suggestions.

Focal points, also known as Schelling points (thanks to Nobel Prize winner Thomas Schelling), are those instinctive solutions that people naturally gravitate towards when making a choice. Imagine a couple debating where to eat dinner—one craves Italian, while the other leans toward Mexican. They could go in circles discussing their options, but if they both suddenly mention "that new Italian place downtown" simultaneously, it becomes their focal point. It's like there's an invisible thread connecting their thoughts, leading them to a shared decision. Focal points help simplify coordination by providing a common reference, allowing everyone to sync up their choices without having to spell everything out.

Understanding focal points is key when looking at how people can effectively navigate different situations. In the café, if the friends were aware of a local hiking trail that many people had talked about, they might naturally drift towards that option, creating an easy consensus. On the flip side, if they're clueless about such cues, they could end up wasting time debating choices that no one is excited about. Having a well-known focal point often makes the difference between a productive conversation and a frustrating deadlock.

As we dig deeper into coordination games, it's important to think about the psychological factors that influence how we make decisions. Social norms play a big part in shaping our choices. In the café, if one friend thinks suggesting a movie night would be more acceptable than a road trip, they might go with that option to keep the peace, even if they secretly prefer the latter. This urge to fit in can lead to decisions that don't truly reflect personal desires, but rather the group's expectations. Grasping these dynamics can help people handle situations with multiple perspectives more effectively.

The idea of social norms takes the discussion on coordination games into the realm of relationships. Whether with friends, family, or coworkers, the ability to coordinate well often depends on recognizing and adjusting to others' expectations and wishes. Take a workplace, for example—team members frequently face different opinions on a project's direction. Here, having a shared understanding of the team's goals and the norms that guide behavior can greatly influence the outcome. When everyone aligns their efforts toward a common aim, productivity flourishes.

Yet, the road to successful coordination isn't always easy. Psychological biases can cloud our judgment and disrupt alignment. Groupthink, for instance, can pop up in situations where people hold back their differing opinions to keep the peace. While harmony matters, going along with the crowd blindly can stifle creativity and lead to poor choices. The challenge is finding the right balance between cooperating and thinking independently. Encouraging open conversations while keeping an eye on shared goals can result in richer discussions and better coordination.

Think for a moment about a sports team gearing up for a big game. Each player has their own strengths, strategies, and preferences, but the goal is to win. Getting these individual perspectives to come together into a unified game plan requires communication and a shared understanding of everyone's roles. When players think as a team, drawing on their unique insights, they can adapt on the fly, responding to the game's ever-changing dynamics. This teamwork highlights the power of coordination games, where success hinges on the ability to weave together diverse thoughts toward a common goal.

In other situations, timing is everything. Picture a group of entrepreneurs brainstorming ideas for a startup. If one person pitches an innovative concept but others hesitate due to uncertainty, the group risks missing a great opportunity. This is where the idea of "first mover advantage" comes into play. The first person to back a bold idea can become the focal point, encouraging others to jump on board. Spotting this dynamic can inspire individuals to take risks and advocate for ideas, nurturing a culture of innovation and teamwork.

As we reflect on coordination games, we can't forget about the role of trust in making aligned decisions work. Trust acts like glue, holding people together, allowing them to share ideas openly without worrying about judgment or rejection. In a trusting environment, individuals feel more comfortable sharing their preferences and working together to find solutions that work for everyone. On the other hand, when trust is absent, people may keep their thoughts to themselves or follow self-serving paths to protect their interests. Navigating the layers of trust adds another dimension to our understanding of coordination games and the psychology behind them.

Recognizing and harnessing these dynamics can empower people to change how they interact with others, creating a space where cooperation thrives. Through the lens of coordination games, we see that success often rests on the interplay of perspectives, understanding psychological influences, and nurturing an environment where collaboration is valued. By embracing this knowledge, individuals can sharpen their strategic thinking, improving both their personal and professional relationships.

Back at the café, the friends have spent enough time tossing ideas around. Suddenly, one member recalls a popular hiking trail they all enjoyed together in the past. The mere mention of the trail acts as a focal point, instantly shifting the conversation. Excitement fills the air as they collectively agree to go hiking, leaving behind the indecision that had previously clouded their plans. This moment perfectly illustrates the beauty of coordination games—the effortless alignment of perspectives leading to a win-win outcome.

Navigating the world of coordination games is a complex journey requiring an understanding of individual viewpoints and the bigger picture at play. By recognizing the importance of shared goals, psychological factors, and the role of trust, individuals can become skilled at fostering cooperation in their interactions. Doing so opens the door to a world of possibilities, where working together leads to success and richer relationships. The café chatter may have been a seemingly small event, but it holds a significant lesson: when approached with intention and understanding, the battle of perspectives can lead to remarkable results.

Coordination in Relationships

In our everyday lives, whether at work or in our personal circles, coordination is what keeps everything humming along. It's that special moment when everyone understands each other, and together, they can achieve amazing things. Think of it like a well-rehearsed dance: every move is intentional, every step works in harmony, and the final result—beautiful synchronization—doesn't just happen by chance. This is what coordination is all about; it's a key part of our lives that can be both simple and complex.

Let's picture a software development team in the thick of their project. Each day, they gather for quick stand-up meetings where everyone shares updates about their work. This brief routine is powerful, ensuring that everyone is on the same wavelength and aware of the team's progress. These meetings create a space for open communication, helping team members spot any bumps in the road that might slow them down. When each developer talks about their current tasks, they not only inform their teammates but also invite feedback and help. It's more than just checking in; it's a smart way to work together that boosts both productivity and team spirit. Coming together each day fosters a sense of shared purpose, which is crucial for pushing the project forward.

In this situation, coordination becomes the backbone of teamwork. Each person has their own tasks, but they also need to keep an eye on the bigger picture. This highlights the idea of shared goals—when everyone knows what they're working toward as a group, it's easier to stay aligned. Good communication is vital here; it allows for timely exchanges of ideas, questions, and concerns. Without it, misunderstandings could easily throw a wrench in the works.

But successful coordination isn't just about having a solid structure or tracking performance. It's also about creating a culture that encourages teamwork and understanding. When teams build an atmosphere of trust, individuals feel safe sharing their thoughts and ideas without worrying about being judged. The software developers thrive in their stand-up meetings not just because of the agenda, but because they are part of a united team moving toward a common goal.

Now, let's switch gears to personal relationships. Imagine a family trying to plan a vacation. Each person has their own favorite ideas—some want a beach, while others dream of mountains or exploring a vibrant city. The potential for conflict is real, as each person has their own vision of the perfect getaway. Just like with the software team, finding a common goal is crucial. The family might sit down to talk about their wishes and expectations for the trip. By listening to each other, they can uncover what each person truly wants. Maybe one person is looking for adventure, while another is after some relaxation.

Through open communication, they might discover a destination that offers both beach fun and hiking trails, satisfying everyone's desires. They've successfully navigated their different preferences, ultimately making a coordinated choice that brings joy to the whole family. This example shows how vital clear communication and a willingness to understand one another's views can be.

However, challenges can arise in both work and personal settings. Conflicting priorities can throw a wrench in coordination, leading to frustration and resentment. In the software team, an unexpected deadline might create tension, forcing individuals to prioritize their tasks in ways that don't align with the group's goals. Similarly, in the family situation, if one person pushes their preferences without considering the feelings of others, it can create tension and dissatisfaction.

These challenges can be worsened by mental shortcuts that influence how we make decisions. A good example is the "Prisoner's Dilemma." Here, two people must choose between cooperating or acting in their own self-interest. If both choose self-interest, they might end up worse off than if they had worked together. This dilemma often appears in team settings when individuals focus on personal success over the team's goals, leading to less-than-ideal outcomes.

Consider a case where two colleagues are competing for a promotion. If they each only focus on their own achievements and don't work together on a project, they might miss the chance to highlight the team's collective successes. Lack of coordination could cost them recognition, as decision-makers may overlook how well the team worked together. Here, the bias toward self-interest clouds their judgment and pushes them to prioritize their own needs over the team's.

As we explore these dynamics, it's crucial to think about how empathy can improve coordination. Empathy allows us to understand each other better, recognizing different perspectives and forming connections that go beyond mere transactions. When team members practice empathy, they can appreciate the pressures and motivations that drive others' actions. This understanding opens the door to more constructive conversations and collaborative problem-solving.

Returning to our family planning a vacation, if one member is feeling stressed about work, acknowledging that stress can help them find a destination that offers relaxation. By empathizing with one another, family members create a supportive environment where everyone feels heard and valued.

Active listening is also essential for better coordination. When people truly listen to each other, they validate feelings and ensure that ideas can flow freely. In a work setting, active listening can mean the difference between a successful project and one that falters due to miscommunication.

Imagine a project team in a brainstorming session, where ideas are flying around like a game of ping-pong. If someone feels the need to shout their idea over others without really listening, they might unintentionally stifle creativity. But when a culture of active listening exists, it nurtures innovation and teamwork. Team members feel confident that their voices matter, resulting in a rich pool of ideas and better coordination.

Trust is what holds all these elements together. In relationships—both personal and professional—trust creates a safe space for people to share their thoughts and take risks. When trust is strong, team members are more likely to own up to mistakes, ask for help, and share insights openly. In a trusting environment, the fear of judgment fades away, leading to a more honest exchange of ideas.

For example, think about a family discussing vacation plans. If trust is strong, family members will be more comfortable expressing their true desires, knowing their preferences will be respected. Everyone becomes an active participant in the decision-making process, leading to a coordinated effort that reflects the family's collective wishes.

However, when trust is lacking, it can create a divide, causing people to withdraw. In teams, this withdrawal might show up as a reluctance to share information, which ultimately stymies coordination. It's like a chain reaction—one person's hesitation can trigger a domino effect, stifling collaboration and innovation.

To tackle these issues, we can look at some practical steps to improve coordination. First, fostering a culture of active listening can help people feel heard and valued. Encouraging teams to practice empathy can deepen connections and insights. Setting clear goals and expectations allows everyone to align their efforts and understand their roles in the bigger picture.

Building trust requires honest and consistent communication. When team members are open about what they can and cannot do, it fosters reliability that strengthens trust. In family situations, open discussions about preferences and concerns can lead to smoother decision-making, making sure everyone feels included and respected.

Finally, reflection can be a powerful tool for growth. People should take a moment to evaluate their relationships—both at home and at work—considering how well they coordinate with others. By looking back at past experiences, they can identify opportunities for improvement, allowing them to refine their teamwork strategies.

For instance, in our software development team, one member might realize they often dominate conversations and unintentionally sideline others. Recognizing this can inspire them to make a conscious effort to include everyone, leading to better coordination and a more vibrant team dynamic. Similarly, a family might reflect on previous vacation planning to uncover insights on how communication could be improved for future trips.

Mastering coordination in relationships is an ongoing process, marked by recognizing each other's views and a dedication to working together. By embracing empathy, active listening, goal-setting, and trust-building, we can transform our interactions. Coordination isn't just a technical skill; it's a social art that shapes our relationships.

As we go about our day-to-day lives, the lessons learned from coordinating with others empower us to build a world where cooperation flourishes. Just like the software team finds success through daily interactions, families can create lasting memories by aligning their desires. Through this understanding, we see that coordination enriches our relationships, deepening our bonds and enhancing our shared experiences.

Imagine those friends at the café again. After a lively discussion, they've discovered their shared interest: the favorite hiking trail. They set a date, eager to reconnect with nature and each other. Their planning shows the beauty of coordination—where different viewpoints come together to form a unified plan, leading to shared joy and unforgettable moments. In the end, coordination isn't just about making choices; it's about intertwining the threads of our lives to create something truly meaningful.

Enhancing Alignment

Coordination isn't just a trendy term; it's a vital part of how we connect with each other in our personal and professional lives. Finding ways to align our thoughts, actions, and intentions is key to thriving in a world filled with different viewpoints and personalities. Think of the process of improving alignment among teams, families, and friends as tuning a musical instrument. It takes practice, patience, and a good ear for harmony. Without this careful tuning, even the most talented individuals can get out of sync, leading to friction in what should be a harmonious collaboration.

Let's kick things off with brainstorming sessions, a favorite in both creative and analytical spaces. Imagine a group of coworkers sitting around a conference table, armed with sticky notes, markers, and plenty of coffee. The atmosphere buzzes with excitement as everyone gets ready to share their ideas. Brainstorming might sound simple—just throw out as many ideas as you can without worrying about judging them—but it can ignite creativity and lead to innovative solutions that might never come up in a more structured setting.

In a good brainstorming session, the aim isn't to reach a conclusion right away but to stretch the limits of what's possible. Each person brings their unique views, creating a rich blend of ideas. However, it's important to set some ground rules to keep the session productive. Everyone should feel safe to share their thoughts openly, knowing that no idea is too crazy or impractical. This sense of psychological safety is crucial; it encourages people to step outside their comfort zones and propose ideas that might seem off-the-wall at first.

One helpful way to improve alignment during brainstorming is to have a facilitator. This person helps guide the discussion, encouraging quieter team members to share their thoughts while making sure that louder voices don't drown out others. A skilled facilitator can also help sort through any conflicts that arise from differing opinions, keeping the focus on working together instead of competing. This approach creates an atmosphere of respect, where differences can be celebrated rather than stifled.

Besides brainstorming, consensus-building exercises are also key to enhancing alignment. Picture a team faced with an important decision that impacts everyone in the organization. Instead of a top-down approach where leaders make the call, they invite the whole team to be part of the decision-making process. This not only empowers individuals but also fosters a shared sense of ownership over the results. When everyone has a voice in shaping decisions, the team is more likely to unite around a common goal, making it easier to implement their plans.

A great method for building consensus is called "dot voting." Here's how it works: after brainstorming a list of options or solutions, each team member gets a set number of dots to vote for their favorite choices. This visual way of showing preferences helps the group see where they agree and where there are still differences. It also sparks discussions, as participants explain their reasoning behind their votes. This exchange of ideas can lead to a richer understanding of the different views at play.

Conflict resolution strategies are another crucial part of finding alignment. Disagreements aren't always bad; they can actually be opportunities for growth and learning. When handled well, conflict can lead to deeper conversations, uncovering concerns and assumptions that might have otherwise gone unnoticed. One effective way to tackle conflict is through active listening—making a real effort to understand the other person's point of view before jumping in with your own. This approach not only shows respect but also helps find common ground.

For example, imagine two team members with differing opinions about the direction of a project. Instead of letting emotions run high and voices get loud, they take a moment to practice active listening. By sharing their viewpoints without interrupting each other, they create a safe space for conversation. This practice can uncover insights that might have stayed hidden. Perhaps one person has a valid worry about the feasibility of a proposed solution, while the other has additional resources or information that can address those concerns. By resolving their differences through open dialogue, they can find a solution that takes both perspectives into account.

Technology has also changed the way we align, providing tools that make communication and collaboration easier, especially in our increasingly digital age. Team messaging apps, video calls, and project management software allow people to stay connected and coordinate their work more effectively. These tools enable teams to share updates in real-time, ensuring that everyone knows what's going on and can address any challenges that come up. For remote teams, this connectivity can make all the difference, allowing them to collaborate seamlessly even when they're miles apart.

To make the most of technology, it's essential to set clear norms for how it will be used. Establishing expectations around response times, communication methods, and meeting formats can help align team members. For instance, having a standard practice for when to use email versus instant messaging can cut down on confusion and streamline communication. By creating a shared understanding of how technology is used, teams can minimize misunderstandings and work together more cohesively.

Setting clear expectations and goals is another important part of improving alignment. When people know what's expected of them and how their work fits into the bigger picture, they're better prepared to coordinate their efforts. This clarity helps team members prioritize their tasks more effectively, ensuring everyone is working toward the same objectives. One way to establish goals is to use the SMART criteria—making sure that objectives are Specific, Measurable, Achievable, Relevant, and Time-bound. By using this framework, teams can create a clear roadmap that guides their work and encourages alignment.

For instance, think about a nonprofit organization trying to raise funds for a community project. By setting a specific goal of raising $50,000 in six months, the team can identify measurable milestones along the way, like quarterly fundraising events or outreach campaigns. This clarity not only motivates team members but also helps them stay focused on their shared mission. When everyone understands their role in achieving the larger goal, coordinating their efforts becomes more intuitive, and the group can gain momentum.

Continuous feedback and adaptation are key parts of effective coordination. As people work together, offering constructive feedback can help highlight areas for improvement and reinforce positive behaviors. A feedback-rich culture encourages open conversations and creates an environment where individuals feel comfortable sharing their thoughts about their own performance and that of their teammates. This ongoing exchange helps refine processes and improve collaboration over time.

Encouraging a growth mindset is a crucial piece of this puzzle. When team members view challenges as chances to learn instead of obstacles, they become more resilient and adaptable. This shift in thinking moves the focus from blame to improvement, creating a space where individuals are motivated to learn from their mistakes. Celebrating successes, no matter how small, supports this mindset and encourages continued efforts toward alignment.

Imagine a project team that faces a setback due to a missed deadline. Instead of wallowing in disappointment, they come together for a meeting to discuss what went wrong and how they can do better moving forward. By adopting a growth mindset, they can analyze their processes, pinpoint potential bottlenecks, and brainstorm solutions as a team. This collaborative approach not only strengthens their alignment but also builds camaraderie among team members.

As we look at the dynamics of coordination, it's clear that it's an ongoing process. The world keeps changing, and so do the teams and individuals within it. Being open to feedback and willing to adapt is crucial for maintaining alignment. Regular check-ins, whether through one-on-one chats or team huddles, provide a chance to assess progress and make any necessary adjustments. These moments reinforce the idea that alignment isn't just a one-time event; it's a continuous journey that requires attention and care.

The principles of alignment can also be applied in our personal lives. Whether you're planning a family gathering or organizing a community event, the same strategies for improving coordination can lead to deeper connections. Setting clear expectations, practicing active listening, and embracing feedback can change how we interact with one another. Just like in work settings, having a shared vision is vital for achieving harmony in our relationships.

As you think about your own experiences, consider how these strategies can fit into your daily life. Whether in a meeting room or around the dinner table, the art of alignment enhances our interactions, leading to deeper connections and more meaningful relationships. The path toward better alignment may have its challenges, but the rewards are well worth the effort.

In the grand scheme of things, coordination isn't only about reaching the finish line; it's about the journey we share together. By nurturing a culture of understanding and respect, we can create an environment where collaboration flourishes. Each step toward better alignment is an investment in our relationships—one that pays off in trust, creativity, and shared success. Ultimately, the beauty of coordination lies in its power to unite individuals into a cohesive team, driven by a shared purpose and common goals.

Dylan Kordis

Chapter 6: The Ultimatum Game—Fairness and Negotiation

Justice in Economics: Understanding the Ultimatum Game

Imagine this: two players are asked to split a pot of money—let's say, a tidy $100. One player, called the proposer, suggests a way to divide the cash, while the second player, the responder, has the choice to either accept or reject the offer. If the responder agrees, the money is split as proposed. But if they turn it down, neither player gets anything. This straightforward situation, known as the Ultimatum Game, opens a window into the fascinating world of economics and psychology, highlighting the tricky balance between fairness and self-interest that shapes so much of how we interact with others.

The Ultimatum Game was created by economists in the late 1980s to dive deeper into the complexities of human behavior that go beyond the strict rules of classical economics. You might think that in a perfectly rational world, the proposer would offer a low amount—let's say just $1—because the responder would still be better off accepting it rather than walking away empty-handed. After all, a dollar is better than nothing, right? But what researchers discovered was surprising: responders often rejected low offers, even if it meant they would leave with nothing. This refusal of a seemingly logical choice raises important questions about human nature and the principles of justice that guide our decisions.

So, why would someone choose to walk away from a potential gain? The answer lies in the complex relationship between our emotions and how we make economic decisions. People are not just cold calculators; our choices are influenced by our feelings about fairness, justice, and respect. Turning down an unfair offer can be a way for responders to protect their dignity, even if it costs them money. The Ultimatum Game shows us that our emotional responses are not just footnotes to economic theory; they're central to how we negotiate and connect with each other.

Think about how this plays out in real life. Imagine you're in a job interview, and the employer offers you a salary that feels way too low. While it might seem sensible to accept the offer rather than stay unemployed, many people would opt to reject it because of pride or a sense of fairness. This real-life scenario mirrors the Ultimatum Game, showing how our choices aren't just about making the most money; they're also driven by our values and the social standards that help us decide what's fair.

The idea of utility, especially when viewed through the lens of behavioral economics, helps clarify this phenomenon. Utility refers to the satisfaction or benefit a person gains from consuming goods or services. Traditional economic theory suggests that individuals aim to maximize their utility, but behavioral economists have shown that this drive often gets tangled up with our emotional reactions and social contexts. When faced with an ultimatum, responders consider not just the money at stake but also the message behind the proposer's offer. An unfair split can trigger feelings of anger or disappointment, prompting a rejection that might hurt them financially but helps them maintain a sense of fairness.

Many studies back this up, showing that cultural differences can further shape our views on fairness. For instance, in collectivist societies, like many in Asia, rejecting a low offer might be seen as a way to keep group harmony intact rather than just an act of self-interest. In contrast, in more individualistic societies, people tend to focus more on personal gain, which can lead to varied outcomes in negotiations. This cultural perspective underlines how context plays a significant role in how we handle fairness in negotiations.

A relatable example is salary negotiations. Imagine a job candidate receiving an offer that's below industry standards. Choosing to negotiate for a higher salary often connects to how much they believe they are worth and how fair the offer seems. Candidates might enter negotiations equipped with not just market data but also an emotional stake in the outcome. When they feel undervalued, they are more likely to challenge offers that they see as unfair, driven by the psychological motivations highlighted by the Ultimatum Game.

Additionally, the Ultimatum Game sheds light on the nature of personal relationships. In friendships or romantic partnerships, discussing finances can become tense when one person feels that resources are not being shared fairly. Those involved might refer to their cultural norms and moral values, which can lead to negotiations that are just as much about feelings and ethics as they are about numbers. Through this lens, the

Ultimatum Game becomes a valuable tool for understanding not only economic exchanges but also the core aspects of human relationships.

The significance of fairness goes beyond just negotiation tactics; it relates to our very identities. For many people, achieving a fair outcome is about more than just the money; it's tied to self-worth, dignity, and respect for one another. Research shows that individuals often find satisfaction not just in the results of their negotiations but also in how fair the process feels. This point is crucial for anyone involved in negotiations, whether in a business setting, at the table with friends, or among family.

As we navigate the various challenges of negotiations, it's crucial to remember that our choices are often shaped by a mix of psychological and cultural influences. The Ultimatum Game reminds us that economics isn't just about numbers; it's about the rich fabric of human beliefs, feelings, and motivations that drive us. The insights gained from this game can help us approach negotiations with a deeper understanding of the factors at play, enabling us to create strategies that aim for favorable outcomes while honoring the fundamental principles of fairness that are vital to our interactions.

Cultural Influences on Fairness and Negotiation

Negotiation can often feel like a contest of wills, similar to a game of chess where each player must think ahead and strategize against their opponent. However, when we explore negotiation a bit further, it becomes clear that cultural influences add layers of complexity, turning this straightforward interaction into a rich and nuanced experience. Culture significantly shapes how we view fairness, affecting not just the strategies we choose, but also the emotions we experience during negotiations. To navigate this intricate landscape, we first need to understand how cultural differences shape our ideas of fairness and the various ways people negotiate.

At the center of this discussion is Hofstede's Cultural Dimensions Theory, a framework created by Geert Hofstede to help us understand cultural differences across various societies. This theory highlights several dimensions that illustrate how different cultures prioritize values and behaviors. One of the most insightful dimensions is the contrast between individualism and collectivism, which sheds light on how negotiations play out in different cultural contexts.

In individualistic cultures, like those in the United States and Western Europe, the focus is often on personal freedom and self-interest. Negotiators from these backgrounds may approach discussions in a more competitive way, usually prioritizing their own needs and desires above all else. A classic example can be found in the bustling corporate world of Silicon Valley, where aggressive negotiation tactics are common. The expectation here is clear: it's every person for themselves, and those who fight hardest for their own interests typically come out on top. In such environments, fairness is often judged by the outcome, with less attention given to the negotiation process or the emotions of others involved.

On the other hand, collectivist cultures—common in many parts of Asia, Latin America, and Africa—place a higher value on group harmony and cooperation. In these cultures, negotiations are viewed as a collective effort, with a strong emphasis placed on maintaining relationships rather than pursuing individual gains. Fairness in these settings is often understood as mutual benefit, and negotiators are more likely to use collaborative approaches. For example, in Japan, the practice of consensus-building, known as "ringiseido," is key to making decisions. Offers tend to be made with the group in mind, and any potential harm to group dynamics is carefully considered. Therefore, a proposal that seems logical in an individualistic context could come off as deeply unfair in a collectivist setting, underscoring the importance of recognizing these fundamental differences.

The impact of social norms adds even more complexity to this discussion. The historical, social, and economic backgrounds of a culture create unique factors that shape what is deemed fair. In Scandinavian countries, for instance, the principle of egalitarianism is highly valued. Social policies that promote equality translate into negotiation styles that favor equal distribution and cooperation. This cultural foundation fosters a sense of fairness that prioritizes equitable outcomes, leading to negotiations where compromise isn't just an option, but an expectation.

To bring these concepts to life, let's look at some real-world examples that show how cultural differences can affect negotiation outcomes. Take, for instance, a high-stakes business negotiation between a Swedish company and a Brazilian firm. Here, we can see the clash of two very different cultural norms. The Swedish negotiator, coming from a culture that values consensus and equality, suggested a 50-50 profit split, believing this would encourage goodwill and teamwork. However, the Brazilian negotiator, rooted in a culture that prizes assertiveness and competitive strategies, viewed this offer as weak and lacking ambition. They countered with a proposal that leaned heavily in their favor, creating tension and misunderstandings that could have been avoided with a better understanding of each other's cultural contexts.

Another notable example can be found in international diplomacy. When negotiating trade agreements, diplomats from nations like Germany may focus on legal frameworks and long-term stability. In contrast, diplomats from more relationship-oriented cultures, such as those in the Middle East, often prioritize building trust and rapport before delving into the details. This difference can lead to frustration, as one side may see the other as evasive or insincere, highlighting the need for cultural awareness in negotiations.

Hearing firsthand accounts from individuals involved in cross-cultural negotiations can provide valuable insights. One executive recounted their experience negotiating a merger between an American tech company and a Japanese firm. At first, the American team focused on immediate financial gains, emphasizing hard numbers and competitive positioning. Meanwhile, the Japanese side was more concerned with fostering a relationship and establishing trust over time. The Americans struggled to comprehend why their direct tactics were met with caution and lengthy discussions, while the Japanese team felt overwhelmed by the Americans' fast-paced approach. This disconnect not only delayed negotiations but also strained a relationship that could have been fruitful. Ultimately, it was their shared commitment to understanding each other's cultural perspectives that enabled them to reach a successful agreement.

To effectively adapt negotiation strategies to cultural differences, flexibility becomes a crucial asset. A negotiator who understands these cultural nuances can improve their effectiveness by incorporating culturally appropriate methods. For example, if you're negotiating with partners from a collectivist culture, try to emphasize collaborative benefits and mutual respect rather than adopting a win-lose mindset. This might involve proposing multiple options and inviting feedback, thereby showing your readiness to engage in a process that respects their cultural values.

Additionally, developing emotional intelligence can significantly enhance cross-cultural negotiations. Being able to recognize and respond to the emotions of your negotiation partners can lead to more meaningful interactions. If you sense that your counterpart becomes uncomfortable during a discussion about financial terms, shifting the conversation to a more collaborative exploration of both parties' goals can help ease tensions and create a more productive dialogue.

It's also a good idea to do thorough research on the cultural backgrounds of your negotiation partners. Understanding their history, social norms, and communication styles can give you valuable insights that guide your approach. For instance, if you're dealing with a team from a culture that favors indirect communication, you might need to pick up on their true feelings through non-verbal cues or the context of their statements instead of relying purely on what is said.

Finally, patience and adaptability are key when negotiating across cultures. Embracing the process and allowing for open dialogue can lead to outcomes that satisfy everyone involved. Remember, successful negotiation isn't just about getting the best deal; it's also about building connections and fostering relationships that could bring benefits long after the negotiations are over.

As we navigate the complex world of negotiations, it's vital to remember that our ideas of fairness are not one-size-fits-all; they reflect our cultural backgrounds. The stories shared by individuals involved in cross-cultural negotiations reveal the subtle nuances that shape these experiences. By being aware of these cultural influences and adjusting our strategies accordingly, we can improve our negotiation effectiveness, ensuring that fairness is more than just a goal—it becomes a core principle guiding our efforts to reach agreements that benefit everyone involved. In doing so, we not only enhance our negotiation outcomes but also honor the diverse perspectives that enrich our global interactions. The journey toward understanding and embracing cultural influences in negotiation can lead to better business results and deeper connections among people from all walks of life.

Effective Bargaining: Tactics for Successful Negotiations

Negotiation is like a dance, where the rhythm depends on how well everyone is prepared and understands each other's moves. Whether you're trying to strike a business deal, ask for a raise, or even plan the details of a family getaway, how you handle these conversations can really make a difference. At the heart of successful negotiation are some key concepts: knowing the basics, being aware of emotions, listening actively, and—most importantly—making sure everyone feels treated fairly. Let's explore some practical tips that can take your negotiation skills from beginner to pro.

One of the most important ideas in negotiation is the Best Alternative to a Negotiated Agreement, often called BATNA. This term, introduced by negotiation experts Roger Fisher and William Ury, means the best option you have if your negotiation doesn't go as planned. Knowing your BATNA gives you strength and confidence as you enter talks.

When you have a solid backup plan, you're less likely to settle for a deal that doesn't meet your needs.

Picture yourself walking into a job negotiation. You really want the job, but if you already have another offer or the chance to look into something else, you have a strong BATNA. Knowing this puts you in a powerful position, allowing you to walk away if the offer isn't what you expected. On the flip side, if you walk into that meeting with no alternatives, you might feel pressured to accept a deal that isn't ideal just to avoid losing the chance altogether.

That's why preparation is so crucial. Before you step into any negotiation, take the time to learn not just about your own needs and goals but also about what the other party wants. What are they interested in? What do they consider a win? By grasping this picture, you can come up with proposals that meet their needs while also pushing for what you want. This kind of groundwork sets the stage for discussions that are productive and fair.

Making sure fairness is part of your proposals can really boost the chances of a positive outcome. Fairness strikes a chord with people; it's a principle that can help bridge gaps and build lasting relationships. When you suggest options that show fairness, you invite cooperation instead of competition. This is where being empathetic and listening actively becomes key.

Active listening goes beyond just hearing what the other person is saying; it means truly engaging with their perspective. When you show that you value their input, you create an atmosphere of trust and openness. For example, during a negotiation, you might paraphrase what the other person has said to show you understand: "So what I'm hearing is that you're worried about the timeline. Is that right?" This simple act shows genuine interest in their viewpoint, helping to build a connection and encourage more fruitful conversation.

Empathy works hand in hand with active listening. It lets you step into your negotiation partner's shoes and recognize their feelings and concerns. If they seem frustrated over certain terms, don't brush off their feelings. Instead, acknowledge them by saying something like, "I see that this is really important to you. Let's figure out how we can work through your concerns." This approach helps diffuse tension and shows that you care about finding a solution together.

While fairness, empathy, and active listening are incredibly valuable, emotional intelligence ties them all together. Emotional intelligence is your ability to recognize and understand both your own feelings and those of others. It helps you manage your reactions and respond smoothly, especially in high-pressure negotiations.

When strong emotions arise during discussions, which they often do, staying calm can be your greatest asset. If things get heated, take a moment to pause and breathe. A deep breath can work wonders, allowing you to gather your thoughts and tackle the situation more level-headed. Plus, being aware of the emotional vibe can help you know when to shift the conversation or lighten the mood to ease any tension.

With these tools in hand, practicing your negotiation skills through role-playing can really boost your confidence. Role-playing lets you experience different negotiation scenarios in a low-stakes environment. You could practice negotiating project terms with a colleague or simulate a salary discussion with a friend playing the employer. The idea is to explore different outcomes and tactics, trying out various approaches to see what works best.

For example, if you're practicing how to stand firm on a proposal, pay attention to the other person's reactions. Are they more open to gentle persuasion, or do they respond better to a more assertive style? By experimenting in these practice situations, you can figure out what resonates with others and feel more ready for the real negotiations when they come up.

Thinking back on past negotiations can also be a valuable way to learn. Take some time to reflect on what happened in previous situations and consider how a better understanding of fairness and emotional intelligence might have changed the outcome. Did you miss a chance to propose a fair compromise? Were there times when managing emotions could have gone better? These reflections can provide insights to sharpen your future negotiation strategies.

Let's think about a specific example: You once negotiated a contract with a vendor that didn't meet your expectations. Looking back, you might realize that your initial offer didn't accurately reflect the value of their services, which led to a difficult conversation. Recognizing the importance of fairness and cultural differences could have helped you offer a more balanced proposal that highlighted mutual benefits.

By taking the time to analyze your past experiences, you can identify not just mistakes but also patterns in your approach. This kind of reflection helps you develop a mindset focused on improving continuously, which is key to mastering negotiation.

In negotiations, success often comes from balancing assertiveness with kindness. Understanding that negotiation isn't just about transactions, but about building relationships, can greatly increase your effectiveness. The goal isn't only to reach a deal but to create partnerships that last beyond the negotiation table. By emphasizing fairness, boosting your emotional intelligence, and practicing through role play, you'll be better prepared to achieve outcomes that leave everyone feeling good.

Chapter 7: Sequential Games and Backward Induction—Thinking Ahead

The Power of Planning: Understanding Move Sequences

Strategy isn't just about making decisions; it's about making the right choices at just the right moment. The order in which we make these decisions can drastically shape the outcome of any situation. Imagine a chessboard where every move is not just a step toward winning or losing, but part of a delicate dance of guessing and responding. In sequential games, where players take turns, the ability to think ahead and predict how opponents will react can be the key factor that decides who comes out on top.

At its heart, sequential games are all about taking turns. Unlike simultaneous games, where everyone plays at once without knowing what others are doing, sequential games unfold over time. Each player watches the moves of their opponents before making their own, creating a web of possibilities that depends on careful planning and strategy. The importance of planning shines through as players navigate this ever-changing landscape, adjusting their strategies based on what they think will happen next.

Let's think about a classic example: two businesses competing in a market. The first company that enters might gain a significant advantage simply by being the first mover. This advantage can show up in different ways, like building brand recognition, snagging prime locations, or attracting important customers before anyone else can. Take Apple, for instance. When they launched the iPhone, they didn't just jump into the smartphone market; they did so with careful planning, releasing an innovative product that secured them a loyal customer base and positioned them as industry leaders. This foresight allowed Apple to not only grab a big slice of the market but also to shape what consumers expected and how they behaved, leaving competitors scrambling to keep up.

However, being the first to act isn't a guarantee of winning. Companies must carefully think about how their rivals will respond. This brings us to the idea of anticipating opponents' reactions. In sequential games, your success often depends on your ability to predict what your opponent will do next, based on their previous moves. Great strategists don't just react; they create a roadmap of potential outcomes.

A clear picture of this can be seen in sports. Imagine a basketball game where one team is ahead in the final minutes. The coach has to think about not only their own team's offensive plays but also how the other team will adjust their defense. If the leading team decides to play it safe, hoping to hold their lead, the trailing team might go all out, trying to create turnovers and seize every chance. The back-and-forth is fluid, and the result depends on how well each team can anticipate and respond to what the other does.

On the flip side, when players overlook the importance of planning and understanding move sequences, it can lead to big mistakes. A well-known example is the rivalry between Coca-Cola and Pepsi in the 1990s. To reclaim its position in the market, Coca-Cola introduced "New Coke," a tweaked version of its classic drink. This choice was made without fully considering the loyalty of its customers and the possible backlash. Pepsi, recognizing potential consumer unhappiness, seized the opportunity to ramp up its marketing and strengthen its own brand. Coca-Cola's failure to foresee the fallout from its decision shows just how vital planning and foresight are in competitive situations.

As players engage in these strategic games, they also have to deal with the reality that they don't always have complete information. In many sequential games, not every player knows what their opponents are thinking or planning. This uncertainty can complicate decision-making. Effective strategists learn to read the intentions behind their opponents' moves, using past behaviors and patterns to guide their choices. The better they can predict future actions, the more equipped they will be to make moves that lead to success.

Moreover, having a solid grasp of move sequences can lead to strategies that use psychological tactics. Think about poker, where players not only calculate their own hands but also analyze their opponents' body language and betting behavior. A skilled poker player understands that showing confidence or pretending to be weak can sway the decisions of others. By influencing perceptions, they can steer their opponents into making less-than-ideal choices. In this way, planning goes beyond just analyzing moves; it becomes a form of psychological maneuvering where anticipating responses is just as vital as making the decisions themselves.

Now, let's turn to the concept of backward induction—a handy tool that helps players figure out complex decision paths by working backward from the expected end result. This method can clarify the best strategies to use at each choice point by determining the best possible outcomes starting from the end of the game and working back to the beginning.

For example, imagine two friends trying to decide whether to go out for dinner. If they agree to go out, they need to figure out where to eat. One friend might want Mexican food while the other prefers Italian. If they can't agree, they may just choose to stay home. However, if one friend knows how to use backward induction, they might suggest a restaurant they know the other friend enjoys, increasing the chances of them being on the same page and having a dinner out. This simple yet clever use of planning highlights how thinking ahead can lead to better outcomes, even in everyday choices.

The ideas of sequential games and backward induction extend far beyond business and sports. They touch our daily decision-making, influencing how we interact in relationships, negotiate deals, and tackle challenges. Whether you're a parent figuring out how to discipline a child, a teacher deciding how to present lessons to engage students, or an individual weighing your options in a personal situation, being able to anticipate others' reactions and plan accordingly is crucial.

As we think about the role of planning in sequential games, it becomes clear that this skill isn't something we're born with; it's something we can develop through practice and thought. Engaging in activities that boost strategic thinking, like playing chess, participating in negotiation exercises, or navigating social situations, can help sharpen your planning skills. Plus, getting feedback from friends and mentors can provide valuable insights into your strategic thinking, helping you improve your approach.

In the end, understanding the power of planning and move sequences changes how we relate to the world. It gives us the tools to handle complex situations confidently, empowering us to make choices that not only benefit ourselves but also encourage teamwork and shared success. The art of strategic planning isn't just an academic exercise; it's a vital life skill that can lead to richer experiences, successful outcomes, and stronger connections with others. In the unpredictable game of life, being aware of how our choices impact others—and how their choices impact us—can truly make a world of difference.

Backward Induction Technique: Step-by-Step Learning

When it comes to making decisions, especially in situations involving multiple players, the backward induction technique can be a game changer. This method is straightforward in concept, but it requires careful thinking that can significantly boost a player's strategic skills. Let's take a closer look at how this technique works, its various applications, and some fun exercises that can help us use it in our everyday decisions.

Backward induction is a method of reasoning where you start with the end goal in mind and work your way back to figure out the steps needed to get there. It's a bit like solving a puzzle by starting with the last piece and working back to the first. It's not just about knowing where you want to end up; it's about figuring out how to get there. This technique is especially handy when there are multiple players involved, as it helps you predict what others might do based on their likely reactions to your choices.

Let's think about a classic example: the game of chess. Each move in chess isn't made in a vacuum; players must consider several moves ahead. You're not just planning your next step; you're also trying to guess how your opponent will respond. By using backward induction, a player can picture the final arrangement of pieces needed for victory and then work backward to plan the necessary moves. For example, if a player wants to checkmate their opponent in three moves, they can start by thinking about how the opponent might defend against that plan. This kind of foresight helps keep the opponent guessing.

To make backward induction even clearer, let's consider a more everyday scenario: planning a trip. Imagine two friends deciding on a weekend getaway. Instead of jumping right into options like the beach or the mountains, they first need to clarify their main goal: to have a relaxing and enjoyable trip. With that in mind, they can then work backward to figure out what steps they need to take to make that happen, such as booking a place to stay, looking up activities, and setting a budget. By thinking backward, they can simplify their choices and avoid mistakes that might ruin their plans.

Now, let's break down the steps of backward induction in a way that's easy to follow and can be used in different situations.

1. **Define the End Goal**: Be clear about what you want to achieve. This could be winning a game, reaching an agreement in a negotiation, or simply enjoying a fun outing. The clearer your goal is, the easier it will be to plan your moves.
2. **Identify the Final Outcomes**: Picture what the perfect end state looks like. If you want to win a board game, think about what that winning situation looks like on the board.
3. **Determine Possible Preceding Moves**: After you have a clear vision of your end goal, think about what moves will get you there. What actions do you need to take to move closer to that final state? Don't forget to consider how your opponents might respond to your moves.
4. **Analyze Opponents' Responses**: Think about how your opponents might react to what you do. This is where backward induction really shines,

as it allows you to anticipate not just your reactions but also their likely actions based on your strategies.

5. **Work Your Way Back to the Present**: Finally, with the end goal in mind, trace your path back to where you are now, figuring out the first move you should make to get your plan underway.

To really get the hang of backward induction, let's look at some practical exercises that you can try. These activities will range from simple games to more complex real-life challenges, all designed to strengthen your backward induction skills.

One fun exercise is the "Restaurant Dilemma." Imagine you and your friends want to pick a restaurant, but everyone has different tastes. Start by defining your end goal—having a fantastic dinner together. Next, think about what kind of restaurant would make everyone happy. Work backward by considering each of your friends' preferences. If one friend loves Italian food and another likes Mexican, maybe you should look for a restaurant with a diverse menu that includes both. The key here is to think about how your friends might react to your suggestions, applying the backward induction method to find a solution everyone can agree on.

Another practical example is found in board games like Settlers of Catan. In this game, players build settlements and gather resources with strategy in mind. As you play, keep your end goal in focus: winning by earning the most points. Use backward induction to analyze what your opponents might do based on where they stand and what resources they have. Think backward from the winning position to decide which move to make first. This kind of strategic thinking can really change the game.

In professional situations, consider a negotiation where you're aiming to secure a deal. Your end goal might be to get a favorable contract. Start with that endpoint and visualize what the ideal contract looks like. What terms do you need to meet that ideal? What are your main points for negotiation? Think about compromises you might be willing to make. Anticipate what objections the other party might raise. This exercise not only helps you prepare for negotiations but also sharpens your ability to consider everyone's position.

The beauty of backward induction is its versatility; you can apply it to everyday decisions, making it a valuable life skill. Whether you're figuring out how to navigate a personal relationship, managing team dynamics at work, or planning your next career move, this approach encourages you to think methodically, leading to better results.

Of course, backward induction isn't perfect. It usually assumes that everyone involved is rational and will act in their best interests. In real life, people can be unpredictable. Emotions, biases, and personal motivations can lead to decisions that aren't purely logical. That's why it's important to stay flexible and open-minded in your thinking. While backward induction offers a strong framework, understanding the human side of things often requires a more nuanced approach.

To illustrate this point, let's consider a real-world example. During the Cold War, the concept of mutually assured destruction (MAD) created a tense standoff between the United States and the Soviet Union. Both superpowers realized that any aggressive action could lead to disastrous outcomes for both sides. By using backward induction, they assessed the frightening possibilities of potential conflicts, which resulted in a strategy of deterrence. The awareness of possible outcomes shaped their actions—considering retaliation and its consequences became a key part of their strategic thinking.

In our daily lives, we can learn from these lessons to guide our decisions thoughtfully. When faced with choices, having the ability to envision potential outcomes and work backward can make a big difference in how effective we are. Whether planning a career path, navigating personal relationships, or engaging in negotiations, the structured thinking offered by backward induction helps you to act with clarity and purpose.

As we go through our daily lives, let's welcome the backward induction technique. By building our strategies on clearly defined goals and anticipating responses, we not only improve our decision-making abilities but also gain a deeper understanding of the dynamics at play in our lives. Embracing this method fosters a mindset that values planning, foresight, and adaptability, helping us tackle life's challenges with confidence and skill.

In a world that can often seem chaotic and unpredictable, the ability to think strategically and anticipate outcomes is a valuable skill worth developing. As you go about your day—with everything from playful games to serious negotiations—keep the steps of backward induction in mind. With practice, this technique will become second nature, improving your interactions and leading to better outcomes. By recognizing that our choices impact those around us, we can use this awareness to guide our actions toward shared success and fulfillment.

Strategic Applications: Real-World Decision-Making

Understanding how sequential games work and mastering backward induction is just the beginning; the real magic happens when we apply these ideas in everyday life. Our world is full of tricky situations that need smart thinking, whether in the boardroom at work or during family gatherings. The ability to see possible outcomes and adjust as needed can lead to much better results. This section dives into how we can use strategic thinking in different areas of our lives, sharing compelling stories and practical tips that you can start using right away.

Let's kick things off by looking at a high-stakes corporate merger that shows how leaders used backward induction to handle many moving parts. The merger between Disney and Pixar in 2006 is a fantastic example of strategic foresight and smart decision-making. Each company was a giant in its field, but together, they could create something that would change the world of animated entertainment.

Before they even announced the merger, leaders from both sides thought carefully about how shareholders, consumers, and competitors would react. They knew that aligning their strategies with what these groups were thinking was key to a successful merger. Backward induction was crucial in this process. They started with a clear goal: to create a smooth merger that would boost shareholder value and enhance the creative output of both companies.

By working backward, they considered how stakeholders might respond. They anticipated concerns from shareholders about new leadership structures, project directions, and the financial health of both companies after the merger. By predicting these reactions, the executives could build a strong story around the merger, focusing on how the combined strengths of Disney and Pixar would not only maintain but enhance the creative legacies of both brands.

When they announced the merger, they carefully crafted messages about the benefits for shareholders, like increased market share, access to new technology, and exciting blockbuster films that would harness the unique strengths of both companies. Each planning step showed a deep understanding of how stakeholders think, proving that strategic thinking rooted in backward induction can lead to positive results.

This lesson isn't only relevant for corporate mergers; it applies to personal relationships and everyday choices too. Imagine two friends planning a vacation together. Instead of jumping straight into destination ideas, they should first clarify their main goal. Are they looking for relaxation, adventure, or a cultural experience? By defining their primary aim, they can work backward to pinpoint the elements that will make their trip successful.

For instance, if relaxation is the goal, they might focus on destinations known for their calm environments, like a beach resort or a spa. Next, they'd think about what factors contribute to that relaxing experience. They might consider accommodations, travel plans, and activities that keep stress at bay. By anticipating potential roadblocks—like long travel times or crowded places—they can make smart choices that align with their ultimate goal.

The workplace also offers a treasure trove of opportunities for strategic thinking. When it comes to negotiating a raise, using backward induction effectively is essential. Start by defining your main goal: do you want a specific salary increase or a promotion? Next, picture what the ideal conversation with your boss would look like. Think about their possible concerns, like budget limits or performance issues. Understanding the setting of the negotiation allows you to present strong arguments that address their worries while highlighting your value to the company.

For example, if you expect your boss to be concerned about the budget, you could prepare a discussion on how your contributions have positively impacted the team's productivity and the company's profits. This kind of planning not only helps you build a solid case but also shows your manager that you are thoughtful and ready.

Don't forget that strategic thinking can improve our social interactions too. When dealing with personal relationships, understanding the dynamics involved can lead to smoother conversations and stronger bonds. Picture a couple facing a recurring disagreement about household chores. Instead of tackling the issue head-on and risking an argument, they could benefit from using backward induction.

First, they should clearly define their goal: a peaceful home where both feel appreciated and understood. Then, they can work backward to uncover the real issues causing their conflict. Is it a lack of communication? Are the chores not shared equally? By predicting each other's feelings and responses, they can create a space for open dialogue that addresses the root problem instead of just the symptoms.

Imagine instead of bickering over who does more chores, they sit down to talk about their expectations and views. This way, they can better understand each other and work together on a plan that suits both. This approach not only nurtures understanding but also strengthens their relationship by building trust and cooperation.

In education, students can also use strategic thinking to enhance their learning experiences. Whether they're grappling with complicated subjects or prepping for exams, backward induction can be a guiding principle. For instance, a student who wants to achieve a high grade in a tough class could start by defining what success looks like—a specific grade on the final exam.

From there, they can identify the steps needed to reach that goal. This might involve creating a study plan, seeking help from a tutor, or joining a study group. By anticipating challenges, like tough topics or time limits, they can address these hurdles proactively, keeping them on track to meet their academic targets.

As we move through life, the power of strategic thinking becomes clearer. It helps us look beyond immediate reactions and anticipate the broader consequences of our actions. This foresight enables us to make better choices, whether in business, personal relationships, or day-to-day interactions.

However, it's important to remember that while strategic thinking is incredibly useful, it's not always foolproof. Real-life situations often involve emotional and unpredictable elements that can disrupt even the best plans. People might not always act in logical ways, and this unpredictability should be considered in our strategic thinking.

Take the example of investing. An investor might use backward induction to predict market trends and plan their portfolio accordingly. However, unexpected economic changes or global events can completely shift the landscape. When such surprises arise, it's crucial for the investor to stay flexible, adapt their strategy, and reassess their goals based on new information.

The takeaway here is to use the principles of strategic thinking while remaining open to change. Flexibility strengthens our ability to handle uncertainty and respond effectively to unexpected challenges.

With this in mind, let's think about how we can develop a mindset that embraces both strategic thinking and adaptability. By practicing backward induction in everyday choices, we can build our skills in strategic foresight. Start by using these principles in low-stakes situations, like planning a dinner party or handling a simple project at work.

As you get more comfortable with this approach, gradually apply it to more complicated scenarios, like major negotiations or important life decisions. Over time, you'll find that this skill becomes second nature, boosting both your decision-making abilities and your confidence in handling different situations.

The potential for transformation through strategic planning and backward induction is immense. By spotting opportunities for strategic thinking in our jobs, social interactions, and personal goals, we can cultivate a more thoughtful approach to decision-making. Whether it's navigating a corporate merger, resolving personal conflicts, or achieving educational goals, the principles of sequential games can lead us to better outcomes.

As we journey through life, let's embrace the power of strategic thinking to illuminate our paths and shape our choices. Each decision we make can have a ripple effect on our interactions and circumstances, impacting not only our own outcomes but also the experiences of those around us. By honing our ability to think strategically, we can navigate life's complexities with clarity, purpose, and renewed confidence.

In summary, using backward induction in real-world situations empowers us to tap into our strategic potential. It gives us the tools to approach challenges thoughtfully, anticipate reactions, and create plans that align with our objectives. As we nurture this mindset, we can foster an atmosphere of collaboration, understanding, and shared success.

In a world that is increasingly complex and interconnected, strategic thinking isn't just a skill; it's a way of living. By appreciating the value of foresight and planning, we can take charge of our futures, making choices that guide us toward the outcomes we desire. So, whether you're negotiating a raise, planning a trip, or simply having a conversation with a friend, remember that the principles of strategic thinking can help you succeed in all your endeavors.

Chapter 8: Auctions and Bidding Strategies—Playing for Keeps

Types of Auctions: Understanding the Landscape

When you think of auctions, you might picture a lively scene filled with the sound of gavel thuds and the excitement of eager bidders. But the world of auctions is much more diverse and intricate than that. While the thrill is often palpable, the different types of auctions shape how bidders interact and influence the strategies they use. Grasping these auction formats and what they mean is key to navigating the auction landscape successfully.

Imagine the auction world as a grand stage, where each type of auction has its own unique performance and a cast of bidders who are just as varied as the items they want to buy. On this stage, strategies take shape, emotions run high, and the stakes can climb quickly. Whether it's the excitement of an English auction, the fast-paced decisions needed in a Dutch auction, the mystery of sealed-bid auctions, or the clever strategies found in Vickrey auctions, each format calls for a different approach. Let's dive into these auction types and break down how they work to help you understand the game being played.

Let's start with the classic English auction, which is still one of the most well-known formats. Picture a packed room where bidders raise their hands, calling out their offers—each increase a bold statement of their intent. This open format creates a lively atmosphere where the thrill of competition can lead to something called "auction fever." As bidders get emotionally involved, the drive to win can sometimes cloud their judgment, leading to bids that go well above what the item is actually worth.

In this scenario, the key is finding the right balance. How high is too high? This is a question that every bidder must confront. Incremental bidding turns into a tactical dance; each raise needs to be thought through, not just in terms of one's own budget but also in anticipation of what competitors might do. The psychological aspects of bidding—like the fear of missing out on an item or the excitement of winning—can weigh heavily on even the most experienced bidders. Studies show that emotions often lead bidders to go overboard with their offers. A successful bidder in an English auction should be self-aware, set clear limits, and have a good understanding of the item's true value.

Next, let's look at the Dutch auction, which turns the typical bidding process upside down. Instead of starting with a low price and letting bidders gradually raise their offers, a Dutch auction starts at a high price that drops over time until someone agrees to pay that price. This format creates a sense of urgency; if you're not careful, you might miss out on a good deal.

In this fast-paced setting, making decisions quickly is crucial. A smart bidder needs to think not only about what they're willing to pay but also how they value the item compared to the current price. Quick, thoughtful evaluations are vital. Timing is everything: if a bidder hesitates too long, they might lose the chance to grab the item. Understanding how other bidders might react is also important. Knowing the market, being aware of demand for similar items, and recognizing who your competition is can all shape your final decision.

Sealed-bid auctions add another layer of complexity. In these auctions, bidders submit their offers in secret, creating a situation where strategic guessing becomes essential. Without knowing what others have bid, participants have to estimate what their rivals think the item is worth. This uncertainty adds an interesting twist to the bidding strategy. The risks are high—if you underbid, you might lose the item; overbidding can lead to feelings of regret later on.

In a sealed-bid auction, understanding your maximum willingness to pay is crucial. Bidders need to do their homework on the item and assess its true value to avoid getting swept up in emotions. Factors like market trends, past auction results, and the item's condition all play a role in this research phase. Then there's the question of strategy: should a bidder place a conservative offer, expecting others to bid higher, or go in strong to intimidate the competition? Finding the right balance between risk and reward is what defines these auctions.

Now, let's explore the Vickrey auction, which encourages a different kind of strategic thinking. In this format, the highest bidder wins, but they only pay the amount of the second-highest bid. This setup creates a fascinating twist: bidders are motivated to bid their true value for the item because what they actually pay is based on someone else's bid, not their own. This encourages a level of honesty in bidding, as there's not much to gain from trying to lowball.

The strategic implications of Vickrey auctions are significant. Each bidder needs to think about what others might bid while also valuing the item for themselves. This requires a level of honesty in valuation that can be rare in the competitive auction scene. Surprisingly, the most successful bidders in this type realize that being truthful in their bidding is the best way to get optimal results. This openness leads to a more straightforward bidding process, reducing the chance of regret once the auction is over.

Understanding the various types of auctions and the unique strategies they involve gives bidders the know-how to navigate this intricate landscape. The takeaway is clear: success in auctions isn't just about the items themselves; it's also about understanding the psychology behind bidding, the strategies you choose, and your ability to read the behaviors and motivations of your competitors. As bidders move through English, Dutch, sealed-bid, and Vickrey auctions, they must adjust their tactics and grasp the deeper mechanics at play. In this complex web of bidding strategies, careful thought, strategic planning, and a solid understanding of the auction's structure can ultimately lead to success on this auction stage.

Winning Without Overpaying: The Art of Effective Bidding

Entering the world of auctions can feel like stepping into a lively contest, where each bidder is determined to claim their prize, ready to put their financial skills to the test. The excitement in the air and the auctioneer's urgent voice can easily stir up emotions and lead to overspending. However, winning at auctions is less about having the deepest pockets and more about having a smart plan. The trick is to approach this game with a strategy focused on winning wisely—without overpaying.

The very first step in any auction game plan is setting a budget. Before the auction starts and your heart begins to race, it's important to establish a clear financial limit. This isn't just about picking a number that seems okay; it involves thinking carefully about your finances, the item's worth, and being ready to walk away if you reach that limit. Knowing your budget is crucial; it acts like a safety net that keeps you grounded, preventing those emotional bids that might lead to regret later.

Picture yourself in an auction house, filled with excitement and anticipation, as the auctioneer raises the starting bid. You look around at the other bidders—some eager, some calm and confident. This is the moment when temptation can hit hard. All too often, bidders get swept up in the excitement, bidding more than they ever intended. But by having a budget set beforehand, you cultivate a sense of discipline that can protect you from making hasty decisions.

Sticking to your budget is incredibly important. It serves as a steady guide through the intense competition. As you place your bids, being aware of your financial comfort zone helps you stay focused. The stakes can rise quickly, and in the heat of the moment, it might feel necessary to push your limit just to win. This is where understanding your emotions comes into play; fear of missing out, the thrill of winning, and the desire to outsmart other bidders can all push you to spend more than you can afford. But with your budget in place, you can make smart decisions, even when things get chaotic.

Next up is the significance of research and understanding the value of the items you want. Going into an auction without knowing the true worth of an item is like heading into battle without armor. The more you know, the better you can plan your bids. By digging into market trends, past auction results, and similar items, you can figure out what your desired item is really worth.

Imagine you're eyeing a vintage guitar at an auction. It looks amazing, and you can already picture yourself playing it at home. But before you raise your paddle, pause and think: how much is that guitar actually worth? Have similar guitars been sold recently? What's its condition compared to others? Having this information gives you the confidence to bid smartly instead of impulsively.

Good research acts as a safety net. When you have a solid idea of an item's worth, you can easily spot when the bidding starts to go beyond what you're willing to pay. This knowledge is empowering, allowing you to step back from the frenzy and assess things with a clear head. This thoughtful approach helps you manage emotional responses that can lead to poor bidding decisions.

Timing is another key part of a strong bidding strategy. Just like in any competition, knowing when to make your move can mean the difference between landing an item at a fair price and watching it slip away for a lot more than you wanted to pay. Bidders need to be strategic about when they make their bids, weighing the benefits of jumping in early against the advantages of waiting until the auction is winding down.

Consider a situation where bidders rush in early, placing high bids right away. While this might intimidate some, it can also backfire. Early bidders risk giving away their willingness to spend more, which can quickly lead to a bidding war and push prices up. On the other hand, you might consider a quieter approach by waiting until the auction is at its most intense. Late bidding—sometimes called "sniping"—allows you to take advantage of the emotions of others, possibly catching them off guard when they least expect it.

So where's the sweet spot? The best tactic often combines both approaches. Bidding early can show your interest and discourage competitors while also letting you gauge their reactions. Meanwhile, waiting until the last moments can create an exciting climax, driving the bid prices up. Ultimately, mastering the timing of your bids adds another layer of strategy to your plan, increasing your chances of securing your desired item without breaking the bank.

However, even the best strategy won't work if you can't manage your emotions. Bidding can be an emotional ride, and bidders face psychological ups and downs, including excitement, frustration, and fear. These feelings can cloud your judgment and lead to reckless bids. So, keeping your cool is vital.

It's easy to get caught up in the thrill of an auction, especially when everyone is bidding for the same prize. Your heart races, and suddenly, logic feels far away. Recognizing this emotional battlefield is key. To help keep your emotions in check, try taking deep breaths, reminding yourself of your budget, or even stepping away for a moment to collect your thoughts. The goal is to distance yourself from those immediate emotional reactions that could push you into making rash decisions.

Visualizing possible outcomes can also help calm your nerves. Picture yourself walking away if the bidding exceeds your budget. Remembering that there will always be more auctions and items can ease the fear of missing out. This mindset builds resilience and helps you stick to your strategy, no matter how thrilling the bidding gets.

Having a clear plan before you dive into the auction is beneficial too. Whether it's a set bidding strategy, a solid understanding of the item's worth, or a trusted friend to help you stay focused, having a plan can make a big difference. Reflecting on why you're bidding can strengthen your commitment to making thoughtful choices rather than emotional ones.

As we explore the busy world of auctions, one thing stands out: winning doesn't mean overspending. By setting a firm budget, researching carefully, timing your bids wisely, and managing your emotions, you can create bidding strategies that help you secure the items you want without sacrificing your financial health. This skillful approach to bidding turns competitors into savvy participants, equipped with the knowledge and techniques needed to succeed in the thrilling and often unpredictable auction scene. Each auction becomes not just a test of wealth, but a true reflection of strategy, discipline, and self-awareness, leading to triumph without the burden of regret.

Avoiding the Winner's Curse: Strategies for Smart Bidders

Auctions have a special allure that draws in many hopeful bidders: the thrill of competition, the excitement of the chase, and the joy of winning. Yet, hiding behind this exciting backdrop is a tricky psychological trap known as the "winner's curse." This refers to the tendency of winning bidders to overpay for items because they get swept up in the heat of the moment. To navigate auctions successfully, it's vital to recognize and understand this phenomenon.

One of the biggest mistakes bidders make is not researching the items they want. It's easy to become enamored with something—a stunning piece of art, a classic car, or a rare coin—without truly understanding its market value. The buzz of the auction can create a false sense of worth, leading bidders to set unrealistic bid limits. A classic example of this happened at a famous auction featuring a rare painting by a renowned artist. Many bidders got so caught up in the excitement that they forgot to do their homework. As the bids soared higher, many lost track of the painting's true value, resulting in a final sale price that was astonishingly inflated.

The winners walked away with their treasured items but were left with a heavy weight of regret, realizing they had paid way too much—a clear lesson in the winner's curse.

Another common trap is the instinct to jump into bidding wars. When other bidders are competitive, it's easy to feel pressured to keep raising your bids, often ignoring your budget. The fear of losing out can trigger an overwhelming urge to win, sometimes leading to paying much more than planned for something that could have been purchased for less. Take the story of a collector who became wrapped up in a fierce bidding war over an antique chair. As the auction heated up, they raised their bid dramatically, only to realize afterward that they had blown past the chair's actual value. The excitement of winning quickly turned into a sobering realization that they had fallen victim to the winner's curse.

So how can bidders avoid these pitfalls? One effective way is to create a solid bidding strategy. Start by setting a firm budget based on careful research that considers the item's value, current market trends, and what you're comfortable spending. This budget should serve as your guiding star, helping you stay calm when the bidding gets intense. It's also important to keep emotions in check. While the excitement of the auction can be intoxicating, remember that you're there to make a smart investment, not just to win for the sake of winning. Picture this: bidding escalates, and your heart races as you prepare to raise your paddle. But then you pause, remember your budget, and take a deep breath, allowing the excitement to settle. By doing this, you'll be better positioned to make smart decisions that align with your financial goals and avoid falling into the winner's curse.

Knowing when to walk away is another key strategy in sidestepping the winner's curse. The urge to claim an item can be strong, but it's important to recognize when further bidding isn't wise. The fear of missing out can cloud your judgment and lead to overbidding. By knowing when to step back, you can save yourself from regret later on. Imagine an art lover who had their heart set on a beautiful sculpture. As the bids went up, the desire to own it started to overshadow their logical thinking. But in a moment of clarity, they stuck to their principles and walked away when the price exceeded what they were willing to pay. While they left the auction without the sculpture, they avoided the trap of overpaying—a true testament to self-control.

Another important aspect of steering clear of the winner's curse is understanding how competition works in auctions. By closely observing how your competitors behave, you can glean valuable insights into their strategies and intentions. Knowing when someone is bluffing or signaling can help you gauge how much others might be willing to pay, allowing you to adjust your own bidding approach. Picture yourself in a bustling auction room, surrounded by eager bidders, and you notice a competitor who seems unusually reserved. This might hint that they're either not as interested as they seem or are waiting for the perfect moment to jump in. With this knowledge, you can make better decisions about when to bid or hold back, increasing your chances of success without falling into the winner's curse.

For instance, at a particularly competitive auction for a rare comic book, bidders who watched closely noticed a trend: one bidder consistently placed small bids at first but suddenly increased their offers as the auction neared its end. Spotting this pattern helped others either hold off on bidding until the right moment or be more cautious as prices climbed. By paying attention to how competitors act, bidders can make smarter choices that reflect a true assessment of value.

The psychological factors at play in auctions can easily lead bidders astray. The excitement can fire up our passions, pushing us to chase items without thinking. However, by recognizing the common mistakes that lead to the winner's curse, bidders can equip themselves with strategies for thoughtful decision-making. This is where research and preparation come into play, forming the backbone of a successful bidding strategy. By knowing the true value of what you want, staying calm under pressure, and studying your competitors, you can navigate the auction world confidently, ultimately securing your desired items without overspending.

As we break down the complexities of auction bidding, it becomes clear that winning isn't just about the final bid; it's about the journey to get there. A solid strategy, emotional detachment, and a good understanding of the competitive scene give bidders the tools they need to avoid the winner's curse. By focusing on thoughtful decision-making instead of the primal urge to win at all costs, bidders can turn their auction experiences from mere financial contests into opportunities for strategic thinking and self-discipline, leading to more satisfying outcomes.

When the dust settles and the final gavel falls, the true winners are those who not only got their desired items but did so with clarity and purpose. They leave the auction with more than just a trophy or a treasure; they carry the knowledge that they navigated the bidding process wisely and confidently. This comprehensive understanding of auctions enhances their skills, empowering them to face future bidding opportunities with a sense of strategy and caution, ensuring they don't fall prey to the lurking winner's curse. Ultimately, the goal isn't just to win; it's to win smartly.

Dylan Kordis

Chapter 9: Evolutionary Game Theory—Survival of the Fittest Strategies

Beyond Rational Choice

The charm of traditional game theory often comes from its straightforwardness. It gives us a clear picture where everyone is a rational player, each one calculating their next move like a chess grandmaster. However, while this model can be fascinating, it misses the messy, unpredictable nature of real life—a lively mix of instinct and adaptation that flows through the natural world. This is where evolutionary game theory shines, revealing a landscape where survival often wins over pure logic, and instincts drive the ongoing struggle for existence.

At the core of this evolution-focused view is a concept that changes how we think about competition and cooperation: Evolutionarily Stable Strategies (ESS). An ESS is a strategy that, once established in a population, stands strong against other competing strategies. Picture a busy marketplace where a particular style of bargaining becomes the norm; newcomers might find it tough to shake up the well-entrenched customs of the crowd. This idea isn't just theoretical; it appears in the behaviors that dictate survival in nature.

To see the significance of ESS, think about the classic example of hawks and doves. This model acts as a vivid illustration of how conflicts can be resolved. Hawks, known for their aggressive nature, engage in fights to claim resources, while doves prefer to avoid confrontation, opting for peace and negotiation. In this scenario, the payoff matrix reveals an interesting truth: when hawks face off against each other, they risk getting hurt, while doves thrive in peaceful coexistence. The interaction between these two strategies leads to an intriguing balance, allowing both hawks and doves to thrive together, each finding their own niche while relying on the other's presence.

What this shows isn't just a friendly coexistence, but the complex dynamics of survival. Hawks help keep the dove population in check, stopping them from taking over the ecosystem, while doves counterbalance the potentially harmful nature of hawks. In short, the delicate dance between aggressive and passive strategies creates a sustainable ecological balance, one that continually shifts in response to changes in the environment and pressures from the population.

This balance isn't fixed, though. The idea of ESS lets us explore how these strategies evolve over time. Factors like the availability of resources and shifts in habitat can change the dynamics, pushing species to adapt in their quest for survival. This is the beauty of evolutionary game theory: it uncovers a world where competition and cooperation are not just opposites but intertwined forces in the rich story of life.

As we look deeper into how cooperation plays out in this framework, we stumble upon an even more fascinating reality. Traditional economic models often assume that people act only out of self-interest. However, when we examine nature more closely, we find many examples where cooperation emerges as a strong strategy—one that leads to shared benefits and improved chances of survival. Nature is brimming with stories of teamwork, showing us that the whole can indeed be greater than the sum of its parts.

Consider the relationship between bees and flowering plants. In this incredible partnership, bees gather nectar while also helping with pollination. Both sides gain: bees get food, and plants boost their chances of reproduction thanks to the bees' hard work. This mutualistic relationship shows how cooperative strategies can develop and stabilize within populations, enriching the entire ecosystem. Through the lens of evolutionary game theory, we can start to untangle the complex interactions that support such partnerships.

The principles of cooperation go beyond bees and flowers, reaching into kin selection and reciprocal altruism. Kin selection suggests that individuals are more likely to help those who share their genes, enhancing the chances of genetic survival within families. This strategy resonates through time, strengthening family ties and encouraging actions that might seem selfless but have an evolutionary purpose behind them.

Reciprocal altruism adds another layer of interest. It implies that cooperation isn't a one-time event but rather a series of exchanges that build trust over time. Imagine a tight-knit group of friends—if one lends a hand to another in a tough time, the expectation of help in return solidifies their bond. We can see this principle of mutual support in various species, especially among social animals. For example, chimpanzees groom each other not just to stay clean but also to strengthen social connections, creating networks of support that boost their survival chances.

The common thread we see in these examples is striking: cooperation isn't merely a kind act; it's a strategic move deeply rooted in evolution. By examining these interactions through the lens of evolutionary game theory, we gain a richer, more nuanced understanding of behavior. Survival often depends not just on individual actions but also on the ability to form alliances, encourage collaboration, and navigate the intricate social dynamics around us.

In this complex framework, we can truly appreciate the idea of ESS and its importance in understanding both the natural world and our human relationships. Just like hawks and doves find their place in nature, we too must find our roles within complicated social structures. The strategies we choose—whether to compete or cooperate—are shaped not just by our own decisions but also by the broader dynamics of our environment.

As we dive deeper into evolutionary game theory, we'll discover how these ideas apply to human culture and technology. The echoes of evolution can be seen in our social behaviors, innovations, and cultural norms, showing how lessons from nature can guide our choices in both personal and professional settings. Understanding these dynamics helps us become more strategic thinkers, ready to anticipate others' decisions and make choices that lead to the best outcomes for ourselves.

In the end, exploring evolutionary game theory encourages us to rethink what we know about competition and cooperation. It pushes us to realize that our instincts, shaped by ages of evolution, continue to influence our choices and interactions. As we peel back the layers of complexity and unravel the subtleties of our behaviors, we gain fresh insights—insights that can help us navigate the often choppy waters of life, both personally and professionally. The strategies we embrace, the alliances we build, and the choices we make all contribute to an ongoing evolutionary dance, shaping not just our individual paths but also the shared story of our species.

Nature's Games

In the big picture of life, the way different species interact can be likened to a vast game of chess, where every player also serves as a piece on the board. The rules of this game aren't set by humans but are shaped by the raw forces of nature. Here, the goals of survival, reproduction, and the quest for resources influence how various organisms strategize their moves. To help us understand these interactions, game theory provides a useful framework, allowing us to explore the behaviors of different species and the strategic complexities of biological life.

One of the most fascinating settings for these strategic interactions is the predator-prey relationship. In this classic ecological scenario, predators are not just ruthless killers; they are clever thinkers, always fine-tuning their methods to outsmart their prey. But prey aren't merely helpless victims; they actively engage in a high-stakes game of survival, using various tactics to escape their hunters. This back-and-forth can be seen through the lens of game theory, painting a captivating picture of evolution through natural selection.

Consider the common lynx and the snowshoe hare. In this ecological drama, the lynx is the predator, relying on its sharp senses and stealthy hunting skills to catch its prey. Meanwhile, the snowshoe hare has developed impressive adaptations; its fur changes color with the seasons, helping it blend in with both snowy landscapes and vibrant summer foliage. This ongoing relationship between lynx and hare showcases co-evolution, where the success of one species directly influences how the other adapts.

When the hare population increases, lynxes find plenty of food, allowing them to thrive and reproduce. But as the lynx population grows, the pressure on the hare rises. Many hares get caught, causing their numbers to drop. As hares become scarcer, lynxes also need to adapt; some may become better hunters, developing new strategies to catch the elusive prey, while others might struggle to survive and eventually perish. This cyclical pattern exemplifies the dance of natural selection, where each species continuously adjusts to the evolving tactics of the other.

Picture this dynamic as a game of poker, where each side has to play their cards wisely and also read their opponent's moves. The lynx might choose to ambush its prey during times of abundance, waiting quietly near a well-known hare path. In response, the hare may develop clever escape strategies, altering its foraging habits or becoming more alert to potential predators. This ongoing exchange creates a continuous loop of adaptation, showing us game theory at work.

This interplay of strategies doesn't just happen at the individual level; it also shapes larger population trends. When prey species successfully evade their predators through effective strategies, they help their population grow. On the flip side, when predators sharpen their hunting skills, the prey population may take a hit. Sudden increases and drops in populations illustrate the real-life consequences of these evolutionary games, with survival hanging in the balance.

But the strategic essence of nature isn't limited to predator-prey dynamics; mating strategies also unveil the intricate games taking place in the animal kingdom. The search for a mate isn't just a matter of luck; it's a battlefield of tactics, signals, and competition, all guided by the principles of game theory. Different species display a wide range of mating behaviors, each shaped by the evolutionary pressures they face.

Take the peacock, known for its stunning courtship displays. The male's extravagant tail feathers aren't just for show; they signal genetic fitness. To potential mates, a peacock's vibrant plumage reflects its health and vitality—proof that it has successfully avoided predators and thrived. However, flaunting such a magnificent tail comes with risks. The more spectacular the tail, the more cumbersome it can be, making the peacock more vulnerable to being hunted.

The female peahen plays an active role in this game of attraction. By choosing mates with the most impressive tails, she is making a strategic decision that affects not only her own reproductive success but also the genetic makeup of future generations. This scenario resembles a payoff matrix, where peacocks must figure out how much energy to invest in their displays. A more eye-catching tail might lead to greater mating success, but it could also increase their chances of becoming prey.

Another intriguing example can be found in the competitive world of male deer. During the rutting season, male deer engage in intense battles to establish dominance and win mating rights. This is high-stakes competition, and strategies can differ greatly. Some males may charge head-on, using their antlers to display raw strength. Others might be more strategic, waiting for the right moment to outsmart or intimidate their rivals without direct confrontation. This mix of aggression and strategy highlights the blend of competition and cooperation, as each male weighs the odds of winning against the potential risks of injury.

Looking at these mating behaviors through the lens of game theory, we can see concepts like sexual selection and signaling theory come to life. These frameworks help us understand the complex choices individuals must make regarding reproduction. The interactions between males and females are rich and nuanced, often involving a series of signals and responses that shape the future of their species.

What's particularly fascinating is that these dynamics aren't set in stone; they evolve over time. The choices made by individuals send ripples through populations, influencing the development of traits and behaviors. For example, if a certain trait—like larger antlers or brighter feathers—provides a reproductive edge, it may become more prevalent in the gene pool. Over generations, this can lead to significant changes in a species, highlighting just how adaptable life can be.

You might wonder if the principles of evolutionary game theory apply beyond the animal kingdom. The answer is a clear yes.

Humans, too, engage in a variety of strategic interactions that echo the complexities found in nature. From our relationships to economic transactions, the same underlying principles of competition and cooperation are at play. The strategies we use to pursue resources, form partnerships, and establish social standing resonate strongly with the patterns seen in predator-prey dynamics and mating behaviors.

In our interconnected lives, grasping these strategic interactions becomes crucial. Just as animals adjust to the behaviors of others, we also navigate a world where our choices affect not just our success but also the success of those around us. The dynamics of cooperation and competition are very much alive in our daily lives, influencing everything from workplace relationships to community interactions.

As we reflect on the intricate games of nature, it becomes apparent that game theory offers a powerful way to understand the behavior of all living beings. Whether in the wild or within the complexities of human society, our survival often relies on our ability to adapt, strategize, and engage with the many players in our environment.

Through these examples, we start to appreciate the richness of nature's games. The interactions between predator and prey, the rituals of courtship, and the strategic decisions we make in our own lives all reveal a world connected by complex relationships, each one a tale of evolution shaped by millions of years of adaptation. Ultimately, one thing remains clear: in the game of life, every move matters.

Social Evolution

As we explore the complex world of human society, the ways we connect and grow culturally tell a fascinating story. Just like the interactions we see in nature, the dynamics of our social life can be examined through the lens of evolutionary game theory. This approach helps us discover the hidden strategies that influence our behaviors, institutions, and technologies. The cultural changes we experience are not isolated events; they arise from a rich mix of cooperation, competition, and adaptation, driven by the technologies we create and the social standards we establish.

When we think about how culture changes alongside technology, we find ourselves in an intriguing game involving many players: individuals, companies, and even whole countries. Each player brings different strategies, resources, and motivations to the table. The technological landscape becomes the arena where various innovations compete for attention and dominance. The rise of new technologies isn't simply a matter of luck or individual brilliance; it's the result of strategic interactions shaped by market forces and the ever-changing preferences of consumers.

Take the tech industry, for example, where innovation happens at lightning speed. Companies like Apple and Samsung are prime examples of this competitive game. These giants are always trying to outdo each other, rolling out cutting-edge products that attract consumers. Here, success is not only about individual creativity but also about understanding the competitive environment. The launch of the iPhone wasn't just a brilliant idea; it was a strategic choice that changed mobile communication forever and opened the door to a new era of smartphones. Samsung quickly followed suit by introducing its own line of devices with unique features, demonstrating how competition fuels technological growth.

This dynamic can be looked at through game theory, where companies act like players striving to maximize their benefits. Each choice made by one player can affect the potential moves of others. When one company invests in a groundbreaking technology, it can shift what consumers want, forcing competitors to innovate or risk getting left behind. This illustrates how cooperation and competition coexist in a strategic game. Companies often form alliances to pool resources, share knowledge, and create synergies that drive technological progress. These partnerships can be seen as collaborative strategies that lead to mutual benefits and propel innovation forward.

Consider the trend toward open-source software in the tech industry. Companies like Google have embraced this collaborative approach to spark new ideas while still benefiting from competition. By allowing developers worldwide to contribute to projects like Android, Google speeds up the development of its operating system and taps into a vast network of creators who share insights and improvements. This not only makes the product better but also builds a community that cares about its success. In this way, collaboration acts as a powerful force for technological growth, showing that great ideas flourish when diverse minds come together.

While cooperation leads to exciting breakthroughs, competition remains vital for technological progress. Companies often push for innovation in their quest to gain market share. Intellectual property rights play a significant role in this competitive environment, determining how firms protect their ideas. Striking the right balance between safeguarding innovations and encouraging an open space for collaboration can greatly influence how quickly and in what direction technology moves.

Cultural evolution goes beyond just technological advancements; it also includes the development of social norms and behaviors within communities. Game theory helps us understand how culture spreads and shapes the values and practices that guide our interactions. Social norms arise from the collective actions of individuals within a community, influenced by shared experiences, historical events, and the context of the times. These norms dictate how we relate to one another, what we prioritize, and how we respond in various situations.

For example, let's look at how workplace culture has changed in recent years. With remote work becoming more common—thanks to advancements in communication technology—traditional expectations around office attendance and working hours are shifting. We can see how technology plays a role in cultural transformation. Many organizations are now adopting flexible work arrangements, reflecting a growing acknowledgment of the importance of work-life balance. This change isn't just a reaction to the pandemic; it's a strategic choice shaped by the evolving needs and preferences of employees.

Social norms can be modeled using evolutionary game theory, where certain behaviors become dominant strategies within social networks. A great example is the rise of sustainable practices. More people are adopting green behaviors like recycling and using renewable energy, influenced by an increasing awareness of climate change. As these practices become more widespread, they create a social norm that encourages more people to get involved. When individuals see their friends and neighbors practicing sustainability, they are more likely to join in—demonstrating the power of social influence.

Significant historical events often act as turning points that shape cultural evolution. Take the civil rights movement in the United

States, for instance. It highlights how collective action can change societal norms. As people united to challenge the existing order, their efforts gradually shifted public attitudes and behaviors surrounding race and equality. The interplay of cooperation, competition, and strategic decision-making played a key role in this evolution, showing how social movements can change the course of history.

Modern cultural phenomena further illustrate the complexities of social evolution. Social media platforms have changed how information spreads and influences behavior. Viral challenges can bring certain actions into the public eye, encouraging widespread participation. For example, the Ice Bucket Challenge raised awareness for ALS and inspired millions to take part in an activity that led to significant donations for research. This scenario reflects how strategic choices allow individuals to use their social networks to amplify their impact—a classic game-theory situation of influencing collective behavior.

As we think about these examples of technological innovation and cultural evolution, it becomes clear that the principles of evolutionary game theory offer valuable insights into the workings of human society.

The strategies we choose, whether in technology or social norms, arise from a complex mix of competition and cooperation. Grasping these dynamics can help us navigate our social spaces more effectively, encouraging collaboration while also acknowledging the importance of strategic choices.

In a world that's always changing, where technology and culture are closely connected, understanding game theory can help illuminate our way forward. Whether we are innovators aiming for the next big thing or individuals wanting to promote social change, the strategies we choose will shape the fabric of our society. By recognizing how our actions intertwine with those of others, we can better appreciate the intricate web of cultural evolution that unfolds around us.

In the end, social evolution is an ever-changing game—one that calls for our attention, creativity, and flexibility. The cultural dynamics we witness are not isolated events; they are part of an ongoing story that reflects our shared human experience. By engaging thoughtfully with this narrative, we can help create a future where cooperation, innovation, and cultural richness thrive together.

Dylan Kordis

Chapter 10: Applying Game Theory in Everyday Life—Becoming a Strategic Thinker

From Theory to Practice: Bridging Concepts to Everyday Choices

Game theory is often seen as a complicated subject filled with complex math and fancy terms that seem far removed from our daily lives. But at its heart, game theory is really about making choices when things are uncertain, figuring out what drives others, and guessing how they might act based on their interests. We all do this, if we realize it or not! Let's take a closer look at how some basic ideas from game theory can turn into practical tips that can help us make better decisions every day.

To start, let's break down a couple of important concepts: Nash equilibrium and dominant strategies. Picture two friends, Sarah and Mike, trying to decide whether to go to a movie or stay in for a night of binge-watching their favorite show. Sarah is excited about the latest blockbuster, while Mike would rather stay cozy at home. But neither of them wants to go solo, which means their choices depend on each other.

In game theory, a Nash equilibrium happens when neither player can do better by changing their choice while the other player's choice stays the same. In Sarah and Mike's case, if Sarah goes to the movie and Mike stays home, they might both feel let down, missing out on what they really wanted. But if they both decide to stay in, they might find joy in each other's company while enjoying their show. This is their Nash equilibrium, where they both feel satisfied because they aligned their choices.

On the flip side, a dominant strategy is when one person's best move doesn't change, no matter what the other person does. For example, if Mike knows that Sarah will always choose the movie, he might still prefer to stay in, knowing he can enjoy the series by himself. His best option becomes clear; he sticks with what he likes without worrying about Sarah's choice. This simple example shows how we often navigate our own preferences and strategies in everyday life.

In our own lives, we frequently encounter similar strategic situations to Sarah and Mike. Whether we're asking for a raise at work or planning a family vacation where everyone has their own vision, it's clear that game theory isn't just about theories in textbooks; it's a handy tool for understanding our social interactions.

Take the example of negotiating a raise. You might come ready with a strong case about your achievements and your worth in the job market. However, your boss's reaction will depend on many variables, like the company's finances, their view of your performance, and their budget for salaries. By looking at this situation through the lens of game theory, you can predict how your boss might respond based on what they see as their best interest. If you think about their perspective—like a desire to keep harmony in the team or to avoid conflict—you can set yourself up for a more successful negotiation.

Now think about a couple planning their summer vacation. One partner dreams of sunbathing on a beach, while the other craves an action-packed hiking adventure. Here, the key is to find a middle ground that respects both partners' wishes. By applying game theory principles, they might discover a location that offers both the relaxation of the beach and the excitement of hiking trails. This consideration for each other's desires helps build a spirit of cooperation and understanding, leading to a more enjoyable vacation for all.

Social events also provide chances for strategic decision-making. Imagine a group of friends with different ideas about how to spend the evening. One group wants to dance the night away in a club, while another prefers a quiet dinner. By recognizing that their choices affect one another, they can come together to find a place that works for everyone—like a lounge that serves dinner but also has an exciting vibe for those who want to mingle. This type of negotiation reflects the daily strategic choices we make, whether we are aware of them or not.

Let's not forget the simplicity in these seemingly complex strategies. The magic of game theory often boils down to basic human feelings and motivations. Emotions like trust, fear, and the drive for social acceptance play key roles in the choices we make. Whether it's the worry of being turned down when asking for help or the hope of being acknowledged when standing up for ourselves, these feelings are woven into the fabric of our interactions.

When we think about our experiences, we start to notice the strategic elements at work. This awareness helps us make smarter choices, giving us insight into how our actions can sway the decisions of others. Recognizing these dynamics makes it simpler to navigate social situations, leading to better outcomes for everyone involved.

Strategic thinking isn't just about reaching our own goals; it also involves building better relationships with others. The ability to see potential outcomes and pick strategies that encourage teamwork can strengthen both personal and professional bonds. When we make an effort to understand other people's viewpoints, we open ourselves up to better communication and trust—two critical parts of any strong relationship.

As we go about our daily lives, it's helpful to stay aware of the strategic choices we face all the time. Seeing how game theory influences our interactions can change our outlook, allowing us to tackle problems with fresh eyes. By applying these basic principles to different scenarios—whether it's a major deal at work or deciding where to eat on a Friday night—we can make better decisions.

The insights we gain from looking at our everyday choices through game theory can also help us understand ourselves more deeply. We might discover patterns in our behavior that show whether we lean more towards cooperation or competition. This self-awareness can guide us as we navigate future interactions, helping us approach them with clarity and purpose.

It's crucial to realize that our choices can impact those around us, reminding us that we're all players in this complex game of life. Understanding these mutual dependencies can foster a spirit of cooperation as we learn to appreciate the dynamics of our relationships. These reflections can be life-changing, motivating us to adjust our strategies not just for our own gain, but also for the benefit of those we care about.

Engaging with game theory in our daily lives isn't just about applying academic concepts; it's also about nurturing a mindset that values strategic thinking. This approach can influence our actions positively, leading to better relationships and outcomes in every area—whether at work, in social situations, or at home. By recognizing the strategic elements in play, we prepare ourselves to tackle challenges, negotiate successfully, and create harmonious situations that benefit everyone involved.

As we journey through life, let's carry forward the valuable lessons from game theory, turning abstract ideas into practical strategies that improve our everyday choices. By understanding how interconnected our choices are with those of others, we can take a more strategic path, enriching our experiences and fostering collaboration in all our interactions.

Ethical Considerations: The Morality of Strategy

Navigating the world of strategy is like walking a tightrope high above the ground. On one side, there's the thrill of success—victory feels sweet and achievements shine bright. On the other, there's a dangerous drop into a dark space filled with moral dilemmas, where every choice we make can be questioned for its ethical impact. This balancing act leads us to ask an important question: when does the pursuit of strategic advantage step over the line into a gray area of ethics? Understanding this connection between morality and ambition matters not just for individuals making decisions but for society as a whole.

The ethical side of strategy really comes to light when we think about the competitive arenas we operate in—whether in business, politics, or personal relationships. Each of these areas has its own set of rules and expectations that define what's acceptable behavior. However, these guidelines can easily clash with our natural urge to outsmart our opponents. This conflict raises the stakes of strategic thinking, pushing us to consider not just what we want to achieve but also how we go about reaching those goals.

Take the business world as an example, where strategic moves often blend innovation with competition. Companies are constantly racing to outdo their rivals, but at what price? A noteworthy example is the merger between two major telecommunications companies. While this merger was touted as a way to boost efficiency and improve services, it sparked a heated ethical debate. Consumers found their choices limited, prices began to rise, and the very essence of competitive markets started to fray. This situation makes us think about whether aiming for market dominance, often celebrated as a sign of good strategy, can ever be justified when it leads to the collapse of the ethical standards that benefit everyone.

Negotiation is another area where the balance between strategy and ethics can be tricky. Think about high-stakes diplomacy, where leaders engage in sensitive discussions that can change the fate of nations. The tactics they use can swing from honest collaboration to clever manipulation, often making it hard to tell where persuasion ends and coercion begins. The term "diplomatic pressure" may sound harmless, but it often hides a messy ethical situation. Leaders may wrestle with whether the end justifies the means: if manipulating an ally's weaknesses gets a favorable result, does it compromise the integrity of the whole negotiation?

Looking back at history provides clear examples of the fallout from such strategic choices. The Treaty of Versailles, for instance, aimed to bring peace after World War I. However, the tactics used by the major powers were driven by self-interest, often ignoring fair solutions. The consequences—growing resentment and economic struggles—eventually helped spark World War II. This shows how ethical concerns in strategic decision-making can have dire results; what started as an effort to gain an advantage turned into a disaster.

When we explore these historical examples, we encounter moral dilemmas that encourage us to reflect and think critically. Is it okay to put our competitive edge ahead of others' well-being? How do we balance our ambition with the potential harm it might cause? The challenge is to create a mindset that weaves ethical considerations into our strategic approach, prompting us to focus not just on the outcomes we desire but also on the integrity of the ways we pursue them.

Ethics in strategy isn't just a theoretical idea; it can be woven into our decision-making processes. One useful way to do this is through ongoing conversations with stakeholders—those who might be impacted by our choices. This opens up new perspectives and helps us understand the potential effects of our strategies better. Engaging in these dialogues promotes transparency and accountability, allowing us to navigate the tricky waters of ethical decision-making with clearer vision and purpose.

Having these discussions can also shed light on how our motivations significantly influence the ethical aspects of our strategies. Are we driven solely by the need for personal gain, or are we genuinely trying to make a positive difference in our community and environment? This distinction can be subtle but is incredibly important. For example, leaders in companies that emphasize corporate social responsibility often find themselves facing tough strategic decisions. Their commitment to ethical practices may lead to short-term challenges, like higher costs, but in the long run, these choices can build loyalty, enhance brand reputation, and create trust among consumers and employees.

This brings us to another important question: how do we measure success? In a world focused on numbers and results, it's easy to think of success only in terms of money or winning against competitors. However, a broader view takes into account the long-term impacts of our strategies on society and the environment. The rise of social entrepreneurship shows this change in thinking. Businesses that aim to make a profit while tackling social issues challenge the traditional ideas of success. They prove that ethical considerations can go hand-in-hand with strategic ambitions, ultimately leading to sustainable growth and a positive impact on society.

The ethical implications of strategy extend beyond individual choices; they shape cultures, industries, and even entire societies. As we see more corporate ethics programs, whistleblower protections, and measures for public accountability, it's clear that there is growing awareness of the need for ethical behavior in strategic decision-making. Consumer awareness about ethical practices has also pushed companies to rethink their strategies, realizing that long-term success now involves not just beating the competition but also upholding values that resonate with their audiences.

In the end, the challenge lies in finding a balance between ambition and integrity. The world of strategy is full of chances to innovate, compete, and excel, but each choice carries ethical weight that we can't afford to overlook. By including ethical considerations in our strategic thinking, we not only improve our decision-making abilities but also help create a fairer and more just society.

Reflecting on our own strategic choices makes us examine our motives closely. Are we forming partnerships based on mutual respect and understanding, or are we trying to manipulate circumstances for our own advantage? This kind of self-reflection helps ground our strategies in integrity and purpose, reminding us that the legacy we leave behind isn't just about our accomplishments but also about the ethical standards we uphold throughout our journeys.

Ultimately, strategy is a dynamic mix of vision, ambition, and ethical responsibility. It reminds us that while the road to success may be filled with opportunities, it also presents ethical crossroads that challenge us to think about our values and motivations. When we choose to weave ethics into our strategic thinking, we set the stage for a future that values integrity just as much as achievement—a future where the quest for success is closely linked to the moral compass guiding our choices.

Cultivating Strategic Insight: Developing a Strategic Mindset

Life often feels like a grand chess game, where every move can lead to either victory or loss, and the stakes are often higher than merely winning a match. We juggle relationships, careers, and personal goals with an innate desire to outsmart others and ultimately find success. But how do we develop a mindset that not only seeks success but does so in a thoughtful and informed manner? The principles of game theory can offer us a captivating perspective on strategic thinking, giving us the tools we need to sharpen our insights and improve our decision-making in every aspect of life.

At its heart, building a strategic mindset is much like training a muscle; it takes regular practice, reflection, and a willingness to learn from both our successes and our mistakes. Picture yourself standing at a crossroads, where each path leads to different outcomes. Each choice represents a unique situation—a game—where understanding what drives others can give you an edge. By embracing game theory ideas, we can enhance our understanding of these dynamics, allowing us to make more thoughtful choices.

One of the best ways to develop strategic insight is by keeping a journal. Writing things down can help clarify our thoughts and analyze past interactions. Imagine setting aside a few minutes each day to reflect on the important decisions you've faced, how you tackled them, and what the results were. What motivated the people involved? Did they view you as a friend or a rival? This exercise not only boosts self-awareness but also encourages us to critically evaluate how our actions affect others.

In your journal, try to ask yourself specific questions. What were the stakes in that negotiation? Were you aware of the other party's goals, or were you just focused on your own? By breaking down these real-life scenarios, you'll gain insights that can help you in future interactions, allowing you to anticipate reactions and adjust your strategies accordingly. The beauty of this practice lies in its ability to turn experiences into valuable lessons, helping you build a habit of strategic thinking that feels second nature.

Role-playing different scenarios can also be an excellent way to sharpen your negotiation skills. Picture this: you sit down with a friend, colleague, or mentor and create hypothetical situations that require negotiation. Maybe you're discussing the price of a car or the terms of a business deal. By stepping into the shoes of various participants, you can explore different strategies and outcomes, trying out various approaches without any real-world risks. This hands-on learning opens your mind to new possibilities, giving you the confidence to tackle real-life negotiations with a sharper strategy.

While you practice your negotiation skills, it's crucial to keep in mind the bigger picture surrounding these interactions. Mindfulness means being present and aware of what's happening around you. In the heat of a negotiation, emotions can run high, and it's easy to lose sight of the larger context. Mindfulness techniques, like taking deep breaths or pausing for a moment, can help you stay focused and improve your ability to read the room. By being aware of body language, tone, and even the unspoken nuances in conversations, you can gain valuable insights that will shape your strategies.

To further enhance our strategic mindset, we can use decision-making frameworks that incorporate game theory principles. These frameworks help us spot potential competitors and collaborators in various situations while allowing us to weigh trade-offs and anticipate reactions. For example, when making a significant decision, you can create a chart outlining different scenarios and the possible reactions from those involved. This method clarifies your thought process and reveals the complexities of your choices—because every decision has a ripple effect.

Imagine you have a job offer from two different companies, each with its own set of advantages and challenges. By using a decision matrix, you can weigh factors like salary, company culture, growth opportunities, and how well each aligns with your values. This exercise encourages you to think beyond immediate benefits and consider the long-term effects of your choice. What will your relationships with colleagues look like? How will your career path change? This structured approach to decision-making strengthens your strategic thinking and helps you navigate the intricate dynamics of human relationships.

Additionally, as we develop our strategic insight, we should recognize that collaboration can be just as powerful as competition. Game theory emphasizes understanding the relationships between different players in any situation, and this idea can be applied to our daily lives. Consider how teamwork can create a win-win outcome—where both sides achieve their goals instead of merely trying to outsmart one another. Engaging in open discussions with colleagues or peers can lead to insightful exchanges that help shape our strategies and deepen our understanding of shared objectives.

It's also important to keep the ethical aspects of our decisions at the forefront of our strategic mindset. As we enhance our strategic thinking abilities, we must remain aware of the potential impacts our choices may have on others. Adopting principles of fairness, transparency, and accountability helps us build partnerships based on trust rather than manipulation. By promoting an environment of collaboration and ethical decision-making, we not only improve our own strategies but also contribute to a culture of integrity that benefits everyone involved.

Anecdotes often remind us of the complexities of strategy in the real world. Take the story of a young entrepreneur looking to launch a tech startup. Initially, she focused solely on beating her competitors, but soon realized that forming alliances with complementary businesses could lead to better results. By adopting a strategic mindset that emphasized collaboration, she could pool resources, share knowledge, and ultimately create a product that exceeded her original vision. This experience shows how transformative strategic thinking can be, illustrating that reevaluating competition can lead to groundbreaking success through partnership.

Throughout this process, we should remember that developing a strategic mindset is an ongoing journey. Every interaction presents an opportunity to refine our skills, deepen our understanding, and reassess our motivations. The more we engage in reflective practices, role-playing scenarios, and structured decision-making, the more skilled we'll become at navigating the complexities of human behavior and relationships.

As we enhance our strategic abilities, we may find ourselves better prepared to face challenges with confidence and clarity. Instead of avoiding tough conversations or tricky situations, we can view them as chances for growth. The principles of game theory can serve as our guide, steering our choices with purpose and insight.

Ultimately, embracing a strategic mindset goes beyond personal gain; it's about creating a life filled with awareness, ethics, and collaboration. By incorporating these elements into our daily routines, we can navigate the complexities of human interactions with intention and foresight. The strategic choices we make today will shape the relationships, successes, and legacies we leave behind. So, let's commit to becoming strategic thinkers, dedicated to cultivating insights that empower both ourselves and those around us on this remarkable journey through life.

Dylan Kordis

www.ingramcontent.com/pod-product-compliance
Lightning Source LLC
Chambersburg PA
CBHW031619210526
45464CB00004B/1657